Raising your Children

IN AN UNGODLY WORLD

MARY RONAN

This book is a companion resource to the video series
Raising Your Children in an Ungodly World
with Mary Ronan
which may be purchased at www.visionvideo.com

Mary Ronan may be contacted at
13 Longmeadow Hill Road
Brookfield, CT 06804
e-mail: lovingforlife@hotmail.com

© 2001 Vision Video
Published by Vision Video.

Unless otherwise noted, Scripture quotations are from the New
King James Version. Copyright © 1982 Thomas Nelson, Inc.
Scripture quotation indicated by NIV is from the Holy Bible,
New International Version. Copyright © 1973, 1978, 1984
International Bible Society. Used by permission of Zondervan
Bible Publishers.

Cover design by Gallison Design

Library of Congress Control Number: 2001094665

ISBN: 1-56364-535-1

This book is dedicated with love and gratitude
to my family:

to my parents, who raised me up in the way I should go
and
to my husband and children for sharing this
wonderful path God has laid down for us.

Acknowledgments

There are so many people to thank for supporting this ministry and providing the necessary skills and abilities to make this project happen. Thank you: Bill Curtis, for your seemingly unlimited support for this project; Ron Harrison, for helping a speaker sound like a writer; Marty Milkovich, Joan Mack and the United Way for supporting the work in the churches so many years ago; the DRE's who were willing to try a new concept and continue to provide prayer and encouragement; Mary Shaughnessey, Sr. Ann McCarthy, Sr. Joan Brennan, Joan Marschall, Maggie Curran, MaryLou Vaughn, and Trish Roccuzzo for answering my prayer; all the teachers, principals, students and parents who participate in my program for your honesty, your questions, your concerns, and your prayers.

Mary Ronan

Table of Contents

I loved God also but not first—just also. . . . God was the big brother I would turn to in times of need. When things were going well, I just went along my own way.

1

GOD, the Beginning

Fifteen years ago, I was a young mother, loving my little two year old, my husband, my mom and dad, my siblings and my life. I loved God also but not first—just also. I was a registered nurse and had a job that I enjoyed, teaching women before labor and after they gave birth. I was an irregular attendee at mass, and I mostly just prayed when I needed or wanted something. God was the big brother I would turn to in times of need. When things were going well, I just went along my own way.

In order to do my job, I had to read all the charts of the women who delivered a baby in our hospital. This hospital was on the "gold coast" of Connecticut, a medium-sized teaching hospital. While many of the women who delivered babies here were urban and poor, the majority of women were of some privilege—married in their late twenties to early thirties with professional jobs and a college education. I noticed that many of these women had lengthy abortion histories—six, eight, thirteen abortions! I was stunned; I was really surprised by how many women had had this experience.

This is the first time the abortion issue became so close to me. I am pro-life. I had gone to Catholic school through nursing school and college; then I worked at Catholic hospitals. I had no idea of the extent of the problem. Because of my personality, I knew what I wouldn't be able to do, but I didn't know myself well enough to know how I could help. Even though I went to church—sometimes—I really had just a mustard seed of faith. But I said a little prayer: "God, is there anything you'd like me to do about abortion?" Little did I know at that time what His answer would be or the path He would take me on to get there.

"Be Still, and Know"

As God often does, He had me wait where I was. He knew I wasn't ready to do His work yet. I had not yet started to try to live the Scripture verse, "Be still, and know that I am God (Psalm 46:10)." I didn't even know He had work planned for me! I was about to learn that God has perfect timing. If we wait on Him, He will be sure our life events move us in the right direction—His direction. So I stayed at my hospital and continued my job.

I taught Lamaze, moved from one town to another and began to teach Lamaze at two other local hospitals. I still was concerned about abortion but was also noticing something else: in Lamaze I never saw a teen. I thought I knew why. Imagine being 15 and in Lamaze class. All these happy couples are sitting together, getting ready to have their baby. The picture is so different for a teen—I thought it would be a nightmare.

During this time, The United Way of Northern Fairfield County started the Greater Danbury Adolescent Pregnancy Project (GDAPP). So still having no idea that this was all part of God's plan for me, I volunteered to teach pregnant girls Lamaze. A generous and giving teacher at a very large, local high school invited me in for her pregnant students. I walked into the high school classroom with my posters and bags. We were going to do a little panting and puffing, and these girls were going to get ready for labor. We never even got started! I was worried about teen moms not being prepared for labor because they didn't attend Lamaze classes. I didn't understand that labor was the least of their concerns. As a matter of fact, labor was so far down the list of worries, these girls weren't even thinking about it!

These girls had no idea they had a place in their body called the uterus. One of the girls thought the baby was growing in her stomach. She was worried about where her food was landing! They weren't sure which act with their boyfriends made them pregnant. They knew what they were doing, they knew they were pregnant, but they weren't sure exactly how it happened. They thought they were as likely to get pregnant from oral sex as intercourse. These young girls, some only 14 or 15 years old, said things like, "The last time I had gonorrhea," and talked about not even realizing they could say "no" to their boyfriends (who, for the most part, treated them very badly). These young women had taken health class. They certainly had been educated in all the details they needed, but they had not yet learned to apply any of the details to their own lives.

So I spent more time working with these girls than I had anticipated. We had a lot to talk about, a lot more than just sex. We talked about respect, relationships, how women should be treated by their men. We talked about the differences between what men want and need and what women want and need. We talked about being afraid versus being in control, making decisions instead of just going along to get along. We talked about sex, what it meant to them, how it hurt them, if it helped them, what kinds of troubles it brought into their lives, what they could do differently. We also talked about anatomy and physiology—how their bodies work, what their period is, and how pregnancy and diseases occur. We talked about saying "no."

Word started to spread about "the lady who will talk about sex." It was similar to that shampoo commercial in which the woman told two friends and she told two friends; by the end of my first year, I was volunteering for 21 different teachers in seven different schools. So I quit my job in order to be a volunteer, not even realizing that God was still working on the answer to the prayer I had prayed so long ago: "What could I do about abortion, God?" I no longer thought about that prayer, but God had begun to answer it. That was more than a decade ago.

God Answers My Prayer

After some time as a volunteer, I had the opportunity to take the job managing the Adolescent Pregnancy Project, continuing to work with the students who never had been sexually active, those who had several children, and every type of student in between. I worked with other professionals who provided services to teenagers such as social workers, school psychologists, housing providers, mental health providers, nurses, physicians and teachers. Everyone involved in the project was trying, in their own discipline, to decrease the amount of pregnant teens we were experiencing in our communities.

We were all seeing the faces of suffering teenagers every day, looking for an answer to help decrease the suffering. We were launching "initiatives" to help ease the day-to-day difficulties our teen parents were facing, and we were trying to help those who already had children not to have any more. We were focusing on secondary prevention rather than focusing on preventing the troubles that lead a teenager to become sexually active in the first place. We were frustrated, and the suffering was continuing: our approach was not as effective as we had hoped. Our hearts and minds told us to help these young women and men, but our direction was unclear. We were trying to do it our way instead of God's way, and we were meeting with obstacles at every path.

During my tenure at United Way, I spent more and more time in the schools hoping to prevent pregnancy, talking to children about choices, consequences of sexual activity and relationships. Common sense told me that teaching only the children was not the best long-term approach. As a mother, I was uncomfortable with the graphic nature of my conversations with the children without their parents' having any idea what I was saying. So we started inviting parents to a Parents' Night to educate them about our program. Parents didn't come. At one middle school I was about to see 800 eighth graders; only two parents came to learn how their children were going to be educated about sex. I understand that parents are busy, pulled in so many different directions—work, school, sports, dinner, laundry, and church. I am a parent myself. But what message do we send our children when we don't take the time to learn about this integral, unavoidable, potentially beautiful or terrible part of their lives?

What I've learned since then is that my common sense was right: teaching the children is secondary to teaching the parents if we want to prevent any teen high-risk behavior. We parents live with our children 24 hours a day, 7 days a week. An educator is going to spend only a few hours with them. All the services in the world cannot recreate the wondrous affect a loving parent can have on his or her children's decisions. No matter how hard all the well-meaning professionals (myself included) work for a child, we cannot replace the space inside of him that cries out for parental love. Parental participation in the life of a child is integral to good decision-making by teens. Parents count! Whether parents choose to bring their children to faith or turn them away, whether parents choose to uphold certain standards of living or live down to the lowest common denominator, whether parents choose to impart values and moral standards or let their children try (usually unsuccessfully) to find them on their own—what parents do or do not do has a profound impact on the choices and attitudes of their children.

God is in Control

During the years I managed GDAPP, I was growing as a Christian. My faith walk was much closer, and my relationship with God was becoming the primary relationship in my life—I no longer loved Him "also." I loved Him *first*. I was realizing things I didn't before about life, love and prayer. I was beginning to learn that life's direction improves when God is in control—that God, at the center of life, can bring a richness and peace to daily life when we lean on Him. Once I asked God into my life, slowly and surely my life began to change. One of the biggest changes was praying more than I ever had; I started to pray for the children.

I started becoming closer to God. I was learning the Bible, praying about the children, praying about God's plan for me, and trying to discern what He wanted me to do. (I have always wished God would just send me a little note to tell me what He wanted me to do. I find trying to practice discernment to be one of the great challenges of living a Christian life.) I knew He had things to say to all of us about relationships and about choices involving the gift of sexuality, but I wasn't able to bring any of that to a public school environment. (The school I mentioned above with only two parents coming is the same school where I brought my Bible into class, and as soon as I walked into the classroom with it a young boy said, "Is that a Bible? It's against the law for you to read to us from that, you know.") God is in the details of our daily decision-making; He is in the details of our choices about relationships and behaviors that we have with each other. He gives us specific, clear guidelines about our treatment of each other. I wanted to bring that message to the children and their parents. I believed then, and know now without question, that God can make all the difference.

That being said, I still thought my job with these children was about sex. That is what had brought me to the children, and that is the subject that still gets their attention the fastest. Little did I know that God thought my job with these children wasn't about sex but was about Him. One night while I was praying, it dawned on me that the place to talk to the children is in the churches. That would accomplish two objectives: (1) talking about God's message for our sexual selves would be expected and embraced, not rebuffed; also

(2) maybe the parents would come. I asked the United Way if they would support work in the churches to help get the parents involved. The United Way agreed to one year of support. So I went to my home church, St. Joseph's in Brookfield, to see if they would be willing to try a Christian sex education program. They graciously agreed to try. It's hard for your home church to say "no," especially when God is in control. But little did we know at the time what we were about to start. God knew, but as usual, it took me some time to figure it out. During that first year I saw sixty children and all of their parents.

All I've done with respect to this program since then is pray—no marketing or advertising, just word of mouth and praying. The work all has been God's grace. After a decade, this ministry has grown to serve thousands of teens each year, with about 70% of their parents' participation. The teen pregnancy rate in the community we started in has been reduced by half, not just because of this work. This reduction may be attributed to so many adults in responsible roles coming on board with the message of chastity, from middle school through graduation, and in churches and community organizations as well.

We've learned that parents are by far the most powerful influence in their children's decisions about high-risk behaviors, including sexual activity. I've seen firsthand the benefit of parents who are involved in their children's lives, who aren't afraid to establish guidelines and discipline, who struggle through the complexities of raising up their child in this very confusing world. I've seen the benefit of parents who pray.

This is my witness, the story of what happened when I just said to God, "What do you want me to do?" And He gave me the best job on the planet. With God's guidance, I want to help you "train [your] child in the way he should go, and when he is old he will not turn from it" (Proverbs 22:6). I would like to share with you what I have learned from all

11

the parents and teens I have met over the years. This book will provide you with practical information to help you maneuver through the challenges of adolescence. It is my hope that you will talk with your children, your friends and the parents of your children's friends about what you read in this book and that we can spread the word about God's divine guidance in our lives as parents and the benefits that we receive when we open our lives to His direction.

God Wants Our Hearts

This is not a book about sex, drugs or rock and roll, although we will be talking about all these things. I believe that God allows us to have fear for our children with respect to sex, drugs and alcohol so that we will turn towards Him for help. I believe that God allows us to be called to Him through our children. He knows us well enough to know that we will turn to Him more readily if we are afraid than if we feel strong. We will use these subjects about which we have great anxiety to draw us closer to God and His awesome power. This is a book about God; His expectations for us as parents; His incredible, unfailing willingness to help us in this most difficult job, how we connect with Him ourselves, how we can help our children connect with Him. It's important that we act quickly to invite God into the very center of our family lives. He wants to be a part of your life. He can make a real, tangible difference in the life of your family and the long-term physical, mental and spiritual well-being of your children. Let me warn you, though, that once God becomes the Lord of your life, you will no longer be the same. Your old ways will pass away, and you'll have new ways of thinking, acting, and speaking. Change is scary, but we mustn't let fear keep us from God. God's changes in our lives are always positive in the long run. He has a plan for us, according to the prophet Jeremiah (29:11, NIV), "plans to prosper [us] and not to harm [us], plans to give [us] hope and a future." The only way we can connect with that plan for

12

ourselves or our children is to connect with God. As with everything else we do, the first step is the hardest: reach out and ask God into your life. Let Him be your Savior. That is what He wants to be to save you and your children for eternal life and for today. That is why He suffered and died, not for us as a group but for you, as an individual, all by yourself.

Scripture tells us how to connect with God. We learn from Him how He can come to us and save us. Some of us stumble because it seems too easy, we don't feel worthy, or we are afraid to let God have control. We would rather have it ourselves. I'm here to ask you to move past these stumbling blocks for your sake, your child's, and your family's. Do it now for your daily life here on this earth and for your eternal life in paradise with God. The apostle Paul tells us,

> If you confess with your mouth, "Jesus is Lord," and believe in your heart that God raised him from the dead, you will be saved. For it is with your heart that you believe and are justified, and it is with your mouth that you confess and are saved. As the Scripture says, "Anyone who trusts in him will never be put to shame." For there is no difference between Jew and Gentile—the same Lord is Lord of all and richly blesses all who call on him, for, "Everyone who calls on the name of the Lord will be saved" (Romans 10:9-13, NIV).

Things to Think About

- What in your life would improve if you gave it over to God?
- Have you ever invited God into your life? Do you need to re-extend the invitation?
- Have you ever specifically asked God for help in any area of your life? For example, "Dear God, help me (us) to become the parent(s) you know I (we) can be. Amen."

13

- Do you spend time every day with God? Praying? Reading Scripture? Asking Him what He desires for you and your family?
- Do you know that God has a plan for you? Have you asked Him to show you the way to His plan?
- Are you a positive force in your child's life? Do you have an influence over the decisions your child makes, even influence your child is not aware of?
- Have you introduced your child to God in any way? Could you? Could you get to know God together, parent and child, if you don't yet know Him well yourself?
- Do your everyday actions show the value of God in your life and plans?

Things to Do

- Ask God for forgiveness for whatever is keeping you from drawing closer to Him. That's where He wants you: close. That's how you get there: asking for forgiveness.
- Do not be afraid. God is a healer, not a hurter. God will save you, not injure you. God wants you to experience wholeness, not brokenness.
- Make time for God. Set aside at least fifteen minutes a day, by appointment, to have a conversation with God, sharing your worries and triumphs with Him.
- Ask God into your life—today.

Scripture to Remember

- Philippians 4:13 - I can do all things through Christ who strengthens me.
- Romans 15:13 (NIV) - May the God of hope fill you with all joy and peace as you trust in him, so that you may overflow with hope by the power of the Holy Spirit.

- Ephesians 2:10 (NIV) - For we are God's workmanship, created in Christ Jesus to do good works, which God prepared in advance for us to do.
- Luke 1:37 (NIV) - For nothing is impossible with God.
- Jeremiah 29:11 (NIV) - "For I know the plans I have for you," declares the Lord, "plans to prosper you and not to harm you, plans to give you hope and a future."
- Romans 10:13 (NIV) - For, everyone who calls on the name of the Lord will be saved.
- 1 Chronicles 4:10 (the Jabez prayer) - "Oh, that you would bless me indeed, and enlarge my territory, that your hand would be with me, and that you would keep me from evil, that I may not cause pain!" So God granted him what he requested.

The most logical place to practice putting others first is in the context of our family. . . . The more of us who understand that the family, as a unit, is more important than the desires or "wants" of any one family member as an individual, the happier we all will be.

2

FAMILY, Society's Cornerstone

When my son was very small, three or four years old, my pediatrician told me he needed to go to school. It was time for him to learn how to socialize. I worked in the evening. So I was home with him all day long, and my husband was with him in the evening. He didn't have any daycare experience—no preschool yet and only a playgroup once a week or so in which we mothers could sit together and talk while our toddlers played with each other. I listened to my doctor, but I still didn't want him to go to school. Frankly, we had very nice days together, and I was in no rush to end this leisurely pace of our lives: no deadlines, no times we had to be anywhere, no pick-ups or drop-offs. Our time was our own. So I chose the preschool program with the fewest number of hours per week, enrolled my little boy and off we went. What a trauma! From the very first day, we were both in tears by the time I left him at school. The very nice and kind teachers would say, "Just leave, Mom. He has to know how to separate."

He was four years old! How badly did he need to learn to separate? Certainly, separation will occur quite naturally over time. All parents occasionally must "separate" (church nursery, Sunday school, an occasional date with your spouse). But I can tell you quite honestly that at age 17, my son doesn't have any difficulty separating, and I feel sure that his preschool experience is not the reason why.

When my daughter Maggie was in Vacation Bible School as a little girl, she learned about **JOY**. She learned the way to have joy was to put things in their proper place: **J**esus, **O**thers, **Y**ou. What does this mean in a family? Who would be more important, other than those that nurture us and care for us? The most logical place to practice putting others first is in the context of our family.

Family Comes First

If we all paid attention to this, it seems to me, we would have more intact families, loving marriages and happy children. The more of us who understand that the family, as a unit, is more important than the desires or "wants" of any one family member as an individual, the happier we all will be. We are least happy when our sole focus is on our own happiness. Our children are less and less happy the more they focus on themselves. This is one of the challenges families have during the teen years: how to help our teens look beyond themselves to the world of others. These are the years our children are most likely to be self-, not other-, focused. It is our job as the parents to help our child to see preoccupation with self as the path to unhappiness, not just for ourselves but for those we live with as well. This is not an easy job. It is tough helping a young one see the value of others first as a way to self-respect, not as a harmful influence on self-esteem. Family is the context in which this awareness should begin to occur. It is within our families that we can learn the importance of others while being well-loved ourselves. It is those with the greatest self-respect that can look to the needs of others; those with weak self-belief often need others to look to their needs.

Family Attitudes

God understands the importance of our attitudes, and attitudes are cultivated at home. Matthew gives us Jesus' words in the Beatitudes, which we can think of as the "attitudes" of how we should "be." These attitudes are counter-cultural to today's world. They will be learned by our children only if we take the time to teach them. They must be learned at home because they will not be learned at school, during sports, or in the community.

Jesus gave these to us in the Sermon on the Mount. He wanted His disciples to understand how to behave as a follower of God. He wanted them to walk the path to true freedom. "Disciple" means "follower." If we are to be followers of God, these are the attitudes God would like us to have. Let's take a look at how Jesus wants us to "be." As you read these, try to think of ways these attitudes are demonstrated in your home, in your work life, in the activities in which you and your children participate. Try to imagine what changes you need to make to have these attitudes become yours. Try to imagine how you can pass this wisdom along to your children to improve your daily family life.

> Blessed are the poor in spirit, for theirs is the kingdom of heaven.
> Blessed are those who mourn, for they will be comforted.
> Blessed are the meek, for they will inherit the earth.
> Blessed are those who hunger and thirst for righteousness, for they will be filled.
> Blessed are the merciful, for they will be shown mercy.
> Blessed are the pure in heart, for they will see God.
> Blessed are the peacemakers, for they will be called the sons of God.
> Blessed are those who are persecuted because of righteousness, for theirs is the kingdom of heaven.
> Blessed are you when people insult you, persecute you and falsely say all kinds of evil against you because of me. Rejoice and be glad, because great is your reward in heaven, for in the same way they persecuted the prophets who were before you.
>
> Matthew 5:3-12 (NIV)

God is asking us to overcome our natural human desires and to rise to a higher standard. He is asking us to live peaceably with others, not to get riled up at others' insults, not to travel down the road to impurity or mercilessness. He tells us it is okay to wait for what we want, to be mild-mannered, to love and revere God more than we love and revere earthly desires. These few sentences give us the information we need to know about how to treat one another.

The family is the place to begin to practice these attitudes. When was the last time you rejoiced over an insult directed at you? How often do you act as the peacemaker? How do your children see righteousness in their household? Whom do you show mercy to? None of these are our natural inclinations, nor are they reinforced in our society. All of these attitudes must be learned and practiced in order to make them a part of our daily life. When they become a part of our daily lives as parents, the children in the family experience the blessings these attitudes bring as well. I am a big fan of rejoicing and being glad. One little bit of rejoicing can change the outlook of an entire day, not just for the rejoicer but also for everyone he interacts with as well.

I hike with my dog, Lilly, almost every day. Some days I can't wait to get outside, be in the woods, experience the quiet and give my body the exercise it demands. Other days hiking in the woods is the last thing I want to do. I feel a little grouchy and a little put out that I even have to exercise, but Lilly wants to get going. So we go. She is the happiest dog on earth when we are hiking. Her tail never stops wagging, and she runs towards me and ahead, back and forth, as if to let me know what a great time she is having. My dog is joy-filled during our hikes. She infects me with her joy, so that I start feeling a little more joyous myself. Now I would have to work hard to stay grouchy. I can't even remember feeling that way once Lilly starts to become so happy. Joy is contagious if you allow it to be—even from a dog.

If we look at this from the other side and think about the last time we spent some time with a person who is chronically unhappy—I don't mean someone in need that we can give some support to, but I mean one of those friends who sees every event as a hurdle or believes that everyone is out to get him, always ready to be insulted or angry, never feeling quite good enough—isn't that contagious also? Only when we allow it to be, but I must admit that I am always very tired, a little grouchy and feeling "all used up," after a visit with my discontented friends. Some motherly advice a friend passed along to me stated that people are either radiators or drains: they either generate warmth and good feelings or drain them away.

In which category are you? Do you show joy? Are you glad to be alive? Is your family a source of happiness for you? Or are these attitudes difficult to find in your household? Is everyone too tired, too stressed, too worried, too angry, too self-involved to bring joy to the family? Right now, think of one attitude of yours that needs to be changed. Review the Beatitudes; decide which one you want to demonstrate to your family and friends, and start to practice it. Is there someone who needs your mercy? Can you be a peacemaker with your child or spouse? Choose one new attitude, and try it on. See the changes it makes for you and for those you love. Show your children the "attitudes" of how to "be." Being a role model of proper attitude is only one of the responsibilities of the family, but attitudes do seem to influence every other area of our lives.

One of the several questions I ask every audience I speak to is, "What is the best thing about your family?" The answers are anonymously written down on notecards and collected. Each of these is worth attending to and emphasizing in your day-to-day activities. They seem to fall into three categories: (1) how we feel about each other, (2) what we do together, and (3) who we are.

How we feel about each other

This is the most common response I receive from parents and children. In fact, more than one third of the middle and high school students I see tell me that the love in the family is the best thing about their families. How much we love each other, care for each other, support each other and make it through hard times together are very important elements of family unity. These feelings really do count.

How do you feel when someone says "I love you"? My guess is that those are words most of us want to hear from the people we care about. I ask the children, "How do you know your parents love you?" They tell me they don't assume you love them because you feed them, clothe them or house them. They expect that from you. The children tell me they know you love them when you tell them.

The truth is that no one can love your child the way you do. Let your child know that. Don't let a day go by without your son or daughter hearing, "I love you, honey. I'm glad you're mine." These are some of the most important words your child will ever hear. It is best if they hear them frequently. Even the big 250-pound 6'4" football-playing senior in high school tells me he wants his parents to tell him they love him every day. Our teens want to hear these words every day.

There is a television commercial which has these adorable little children, probably four or five years old, little messy faces, cute imperfections in their speech, dressed to play, asking us questions. We see them close up as they ask, "How much do you love your child?" "Enough to enter a burning building?" "Enough to face a charging rhinoceros?" "Enough to buy a minivan?"

This commercial asks one great question. (And it's not the one about the mini-van.) "How much do you love your child?" Let's take a look at some of the ways we can show our child that we love him. If we pay attention to the important

22

details, our child will know we love him—even if we don't buy a minivan. We have a perfect role model for love in Christ. Jesus Christ loved your child enough to die on the cross for your child's eternal life. What does God want in return for His sacrifice on the cross? He wants us. He wants this child He gave you as a gift to be returned to Him for eternal life. He wants your son or daughter to spend eternity with him in Paradise at the end of this earthly life. He loves your child enough to make the ultimate sacrifice of His life to allow for this to happen.

Do my children know that I love them enough to die for them? Do they know that I love them enough to discipline them? Do they know that I love them enough not to allow them to get into harmful situations by saying "no" to certain parties or other social opportunities? Do my "I love you" words and my "I love you" actions show my child the path to God's ultimate, eternal love? Do I love my child patiently, kindly, and gently? Do I have reasonable expectations for right behavior and allow the natural consequences to occur when wrong behavior takes place? These are the ways Christ loves us.

What we do together

One of the most satisfying answers I see during my pre-program surveys is how many children really love to spend time with their families. About one third of the teens I see tell me they love to be together with their families. They like family parties, movie and pizza night, talking after dinner. They love vacations together or weekends away. They enjoy their relatives. They enjoy shared activities such as hiking, sports, music, skiing, bike-riding. Most of the answers are very revealing about the importance of the closeness of the family. Our culture tries to convince us that children, especially teenagers, don't want to be with their parents. Our teenagers tell me otherwise.

From the time our children were very small, we have been encouraged to be separate from them. There was much controversy over where a baby should sleep: Will you spoil your infant forever with one night in your bed? Should you lie down with your toddler? How about letting your scared preschooler into your bed in the middle of the night? Well-meaning professionals regularly are trying to convince us that separation is not only necessary but also desirable long before our children are ready. Mothers who keep their three or four year old home from school worry if their little one will be "behind" in kindergarten. (Exactly what is "behind" or "ahead" in kindergarten?) Repeatedly we are reminded that the peer group is "more important" once our child reaches middle school, which in many towns happens when our children are only ten years old.

One of our ultimate goals as parents should be that our children become independent young adults. They will need to live on their own, be responsible for their own well-being and have the capacity also to be responsible for others. This is a process, however, that takes time and training. This is a long-term goal that is met best by children who are allowed to be dependent first. We know that an infant who is crawling will be more likely to crawl away, learn and explore if she knows she can come right back to the safety of Mom or Dad. An infant who can't count on a safety system is less likely to explore. We wouldn't dream of letting our infant crawl off a ledge, would we?

Teenagers are not very different from toddlers developmentally. But do we allow *them* to "crawl off a ledge" routinely without proper safety guidelines and precautions? They have the physical ability to do certain things, like drink alcohol and have sex, but they have not yet achieved the emotional or intellectual maturity to do these things in the right way. They need to have the boundaries and expectations from their parents to know their limits. Since it is an adolescent's job to push the boundaries to be sure of them, it is the parent's job to be clear about where the boundaries are. The gradual process of learning the limits, knowing where they are and living within them is the process that will slowly take our child from total dependence to responsible independence.

All this is done within the context of the family. Again, like the toddler, the teen experiences some ambivalence about this. They want to spend time with their families, but they live in a culture that encourages them to separate before they are ready. They tell me they enjoy the time they spend with their families most of all, but they tell me this anonymously, without any of their peers knowing the answer. They want their family to love them, support them and think they are a person of value. They like it when the whole family is together. Family time provides a sturdy foundation of love, support, and the value of family. Don't get me wrong. They want to be with their friends also, but family time is more important to our children than we realize. Our children are more likely to appreciate time with their friends when they also have valuable time with their families. They are more likely to choose friends carefully if friends are included in some of the family time, especially if the families of your child's friends become your friends as well.

We show just how important family is in the way we spend our time. Our children will respond to this. If we make family time a priority—we wouldn't even consider giving any family time away—our children will establish that priority as well. Oh, sure, there may be some resistance, but if this is a family expectation, the resistance is weak and easy to overcome, sometimes by just not paying any attention to it. This is one of those times when your teenager is complaining, "Why do we have to go to this party? My friends are all getting together this afternoon." And all you have to say is, "Well, your friends will still love you even if you miss out on their outing today," and take your complaining teen to the car. After some sulking, maybe more complaining, your child eventually will come around. If you have never made your child do something he didn't want to do before, the resistance will be greater. But calm, patient, quiet insistence eventually will win your child over. Eventually your child will see your quiet way of meaning business.

It bears repeating: children love family events, family parties, family vacations. They love "Monopoly night," "the night we all stay home," "turn off the TV and play games," or some other family activity. Children love shared family activity: "we all play sports," "we all ride bikes," "we all love music, participate in theatre, love to camp. . . ." We should capitalize on this. Plan family activities and outings; get together with the relatives. Stay in, have pizza, and play games on Friday nights. Be together! The years to do this are fleeting. Many of our children will head off to college after just eighteen years of Friday nights. Take advantage of this time together.

Who we are

The third category is some specific attribute of the family, such as, "We are funny." The children love that their families are funny. They love that their family is very big, or very small; they love that their family is Catholic or Jewish, Italian or Puerto Rican; they love that it's just "me and my mom," or "my grandparents live with us." Some children love someone by name or "my little brother or sister."

Children learn who their family is through family history. Tell the stories: "Grandma and Grandpa" stories, "aunt and uncle" stories, "you as a little child" stories, stories about long-distance relatives. Funny stories are especially popular: the time dad fell off his bike, the time Nana rocked the injured duck to sleep, the funny thing Grandma or Grandpa used to say to get their children to behave. Provide your child with the connection to the past.

A good solid relationship with grandparents is very helpful in this regard. Grandparents may tell stories about us parents that we wish they wouldn't, but they are their stories to tell and will give our child some insight into another aspect of Mom or Dad.

When my son Steve was fifteen, my dad took him on a trip to the place where he grew up. They went to his old streets and saw the place he played ball and got into trouble with his friends—places that shaped who Grampi is today. Although I wouldn't have thought it possible, my son cherishes his relationship with my father even more after that special day. He knows where he comes from, not just in thought and word, not just his genes and family tree, but also the physical place: he is connected to his past. These stories helped Steve have a fuller appreciation for where his own life can lead and increase his own responsibility.

Clearly family relationships are important in teenagers' lives. However, I am concerned with the responses I receive to the question, "What is the best thing about your family?" from teens that belong to families of wealth. These teens seem to struggle with this question. But it's not their answers that are markedly different; it's their visible responses when the question is asked. Children in wealthy communities have significantly more trouble coming up with an answer. They are also much more likely to roll their eyes, sigh loudly or do other equally adolescent actions indicating to their friends, "How could there be anything I like in my family at all?"— cynicism and peer pressure in action, both at the same time. Many of the students whom I speak to live in wealthy communities on the East coast, the same "gold coast" I spoke of in the last chapter. Other students I work with represent the urban poor. One school I go to is the largest in the state of Connecticut with 2,600 students, where 42 different languages all together are spoken at home. Another school has children who have to hide under their beds because of gunshots in their neighborhoods. Still another school has only girls, some of whom are dropped off in limousines in the morning. I see children from every walk of life imaginable.

Whenever I start at a new high school, I drive through the parking lot before I begin in order to check out the cars. If the cars in the student parking lot are later model or more luxurious than those in the teachers' lot, I know that I am going to have a more difficult time on the question, "What is good about your family?" When I first encountered this attitude, I thought it was a fluke. How could children whose parents drive them everywhere, write big checks for private lessons, make sure they are clothed in the latest fashions, and live in gigantic houses have trouble thinking of something they like about their family? Why do children who are in foster care, whose parents are drug addicts or scrape together to make ends meet, act as though they like their families better? I'm not completely sure of the answer to this, even after ten years of working with teens, but I believe one of the challenges is time. Though possessions themselves are not wrong, they are never a good substitute for time.

Family = T-I-M-E

A great challenge for families of today is the scarcity of time that they have together. This is particularly true in communities in which both parents are hardworking professionals, more children are living with only one parent as a result of divorce, competition for material wealth is high, the children are involved in a broad multitude of planned activities, and having a social life is considered very important, beginning at a very young age. Last year the state of Connecticut, my home state, launched an ad campaign aimed at getting families to eat dinner together once per week! While this campaign is commendable, once a week is not nearly enough. How are we going to know one another if we rarely eat together? If our children are overinvolved in planned activities, how does that leave time for unplanned family conversation? If we don't have dinnertime conversation, we miss an opportunity to tell those family stories, make each other laugh, enrich one another's lives.

28

A frequent source of frustration for parents is the number of sports practices that interfere with the dinner hour. In one community I suggested a bedtime of 9:00 p.m. to parents of third- and fourth-grade students, and the parents were outraged. They wanted to know how I imagined this to be possible when I factored in after-school activities and sports. If we can't get our children to bed at a decent hour, how do we have time to be relaxed and at ease with each other? We would hesitate to think of healthy outlets as antifamily, but too many planned activities (even good ones) can interfere with the time you have as a family. Sometimes parents may consider these activities, sports practices and extracurricular events, to be "family time." Although being a part of our children's special interests is important, it is no substitute for family interaction and communication.

If you are always entertaining someone else's child, or if your child often is sleeping over at her friend's, it is very difficult to spend the time that's necessary to show her that family is priority. If all of our quality time is in the car rather than at our kitchen table, how can we establish intimacy with the people we love most of all? The importance of family is a message that we have to live. Our children will learn the importance of family only if we show them. Just telling them is not enough.

If you are a two-parent family, then your marriage needs to be your first priority: the center of the family is the marriage. John Rosemond, the author of *The Six-Point Plan of Raising Happy, Healthy Children,* writes of the "parent-centered family" as the place where children grow up to be healthiest. (For single parents that translates into being sure you take care of yourself.) Parents are the power plant for the family, keeping the family going. The parent has the position of power and authority: he defines, leads and sustains the family unit. Children feel most secure and protected in a family in which the marriage (or the parent) is attended to.[1]

I encourage you to do everything possible to sustain your marriage. Talk to each other; say kind and loving things to and about one another in front of the children. Get caught being affectionate—don't forget to hug in the kitchen. The marriage precedes the children and should continue long after the children are grown and on their own. Focus on the positive elements of your marriage, write them down, discuss them with your spouse, be glad for what is good. Pray for one another, pray together, pray for the integrity of your family. This isn't always easy, but the results will benefit not just you and your children but your children's future spouses and children as well. It is hard to sustain a marriage over a large number of years, particularly in today's culture, in which marriage is "thrown away." But research continually shows us the benefits of working at your marriage—for everyone involved.

Every day I see the negative results of divorce on middle school children. If only the parents could see their 12-year-old daughter crying with all the force of a broken heart because her dad is leaving the family, or see the anger in the words of a 13-year-old son who states that his "family sucks" and "there is nothing good about my parents" when asked to write something positive about his family. If parents could step away from their pursuit of personal "happiness" at the cost of the happiness of four or more other family members, perhaps they would think twice about rupturing their family with divorce. Read *The Unexpected Legacy of Divorce*, by Judith Wallerstein, to understand the full impact of divorce on the children. Our children are learning from us how to be a family. They have no other primary resource besides their own family. They will someday role-model what we show them. Children must feel that their family is good and strong. (This possibly may be maintained even with a single parent who stays healthy physically, mentally and spiritually. But every single parent understands how extremely hard that job is.) Pray for yourself and your children; pray for your ex-spouse, especially when times are difficult between you.

Whatever the makeup of your family is, be a family: eating together, spending time together, enjoying one another's company, doing the work that is necessary to keep the family going. Talk about family; express the pleasures of being together for dinner, for an evening, for the day or for vacation; wallow in the pleasures of family life. Focus on the positive, the love, concern and caring you all have for one another, the strengths of the family as a whole, made up of the strengths of the parents as leaders. Be a conscious family: be deliberate in your care for one another, think before you make decisions, and be aware of the gifts that your family has and celebrate them.

Things to Think About

- What is the best thing about your family?
- How can you capitalize on your family's strength?
- What are some positive traits you can emphasize about your family? Do you love each other? Support each other? Do you have fun together? Share any hobbies or activities? Have any private jokes?
- Do you know how your children view your family?
- Are you familiar with your heritage? Do your children know any family stories about grandparents, aunts or uncles?
- How much time do you spend together as a family? How do you spend this time?
- Would your children identify family as your priority if they were asked?
- Do you make honest, loving statements about your spouse and your children?

Things to Do

- Pray about your family life. Ask God for strength to create the family atmosphere you desire; ask Him to show you the family atmosphere He desires for you.

Sometimes you may have to pray this prayer many times during the day, particularly when you are challenged (making dinner, overseeing homework, disagreeing with your teens about what they can or can't do that night, running two loads of laundry, worrying about paying the bills and trying to work through a tough spot in your marriage all at the same time).

- Work on improving your marriage.
- Talk about family history at the dinner table.
- Laugh with each other.
- Spend time together having fun at least once per week.
- Ask what your children like the best about their family.
- Decrease overnight stays with other children to once or twice per month, and do something as a family instead.
- Eat dinner together as often as possible.
- Decrease the amount of scheduled activities the children have. (Do they really need to play two sports, play an instrument *and* take dancing lessons?)
- Turn off the telephone or turn on the answering machine during dinner.
- Designate one day per week as "family night." Make no other commitments yourself, and do not allow your children to do so either. Spend this day together. Enjoy each other.
- Choose one Beatitude to live. Practice it yourself and with one another. Watch for the positive changes in your life.
- Make honest, positive statements about your spouse to your children. Get caught showing affection to one another.
- Make a list of the things you like best about your spouse and your family. Refer to this list when times get tough.

Scripture to Remember

- Colossians 3:12-14 (NIV) - As God's chosen people, holy and dearly loved, clothe yourselves with compassion, kindness, humility, gentleness and patience. Bear with each other and forgive whatever grievances you may have against one another. Forgive as the Lord forgave you. And over all these virtues put on love.
- Colossians 3:15 (NIV) - Let the peace of Christ rule in your hearts.
- Colossians 3:20-21 (NIV) - Children, obey your parents in everything, for this pleases the Lord. Fathers, do not embitter your children, or they will become discouraged.
- Proverbs 15:1 (NIV) - A gentle answer turns away wrath, but a harsh word stirs up anger.
- Matthew 5:3-12 (NIV) -

Blessed are the poor in spirit, for theirs is the kingdom of heaven.

Blessed are those who mourn, for they will be comforted.

Blessed are the meek, for they will inherit the earth.

Blessed are those who hunger and thirst for righteousness, for they will be filled.

Blessed are the merciful, for they will be shown mercy.

Blessed are the pure in heart, for they will see God.

Blessed are the peacemakers, for they will be called the sons of God.

Blessed are those who are persecuted because of righteousness, for theirs is the kingdom of heaven.

Blessed are you when people insult you, persecute you and falsely say all kinds of evil against you because of me. Rejoice and be glad, because great is your reward in heaven, for in the same way they persecuted the prophets who were before you.

Lack of discipline puts our children in a very awkward place—in charge of themselves. Any teen knows deep down that he should not be in charge. That doesn't mean he doesn't want to be in charge. . . . It just means that your child is not ready to be in charge of all of his own decisions yet. Your child needs you to continue to set the limits.

3

DISCIPLINE, the Trust Builder

One night my family went to watch a high school football game between our hometown school and the parochial school my son attends. I recently had finished doing my Family Life and Sex Education program at my son's school, so I was a familiar face to the parents. When we arrived at the game and stood next to the fence, the parents standing next to me said, "You're just who we need to see. We are having a problem with our daughter tonight. Maybe you can tell us what to do." It seems their daughter, aged 16, had a big drinking party the weekend before when the parents were away overnight at a family wedding. She invited most of her high school class, despite the fact that she was responsible for her two younger siblings. The neighbors called the police, who broke up the party. When the parents arrived home the next day, the neighbors informed them what had taken place while they were away.

The parents chose to handle the problem in this way. They had their daughter call up all the children who were at the party and invite them over. The parents met with them and told them of their disappointment, the risks of drinking, and the difficult position their choices put the parents in. ("One of you could have been killed drinking and driving, and we would have been responsible, etc.") They had the teens clean up the mess from the night before.

The practice of discipline seems to be an area of parenting in which many parents of teens run into trouble. Many of the parents I see are uncomfortable with the freedoms they allow their children; they express that they are not sure they provide enough discipline for their children. They are probably right. Lack of discipline puts our children in a very awkward place—in charge of themselves. Any teen knows deep down that he should not be in charge. That doesn't mean he doesn't want to be in charge. It doesn't mean he isn't going to tell you, maybe loudly, that he should be in charge. ("I'm fifteen, Mom. I'm not a baby. I know what to do.") It just means that your child is not ready to be in charge of all of his own decisions yet. Your child needs you to continue to set the limits.

Pushing the Limits

Their bodies are changing every day. They go to bed one size and wake up another. They have feelings they have never felt before, and they don't know exactly how to handle it. From one minute to the next, their perspective on the same issue changes. They believe that the rules for them are changing, but they are not yet sure of the new rules. Intellectual maturity takes much longer, yet they are physically ready to take on new challenges. They experience an emotional roller coaster: much of the time they are not even sure how they feel. Sometimes everything seems possible; they feel invincible, they feel powerful. Other times, nothing seems possible; they feel uncertain and ill-prepared for everything. What they don't feel is in control. They need us to provide some external control while they are developing self-control. They bump up against the boundaries to find out where the boundaries are. But the limits have to be there in the first place, or your child will go looking for them somewhere else.

We want our children to be happy, at times to the exclusion of wanting them to be good. When I ask my students how parents can help with the troubles of being a teenager, the second most common answer is to discipline them. In his book *Saving Childhood*, Michael Medved identifies the importance of discipline: "delineating rules strongly from the earliest ages, particularly rules emphasizing self-discipline and control—provides your children with two extremely worthwhile benefits:

1. Knowing what is expected of them forms the security children need for innocence.
2. Limits enforced and practiced from early ages pay off later, inoculating your children with self-discipline against the social problems plaguing teens."[1]

The children actually are asking us to pay parental attention to them. They want us to know whom they are with and where they are going. They want us to be in control—not punitive, not harsh, not unreasonable, not loud, not unpleasant, just in charge.

This is also the issue they are going to fight us on. You know, the "What's the matter? Don't you trust me?" conversation. We are going to say, "Of course, I trust you. I just have to know whom you are going to be with and where you are going. My job as your parent is to know this about you." They are going to tell us they are old enough to make their own decisions. And they are right; they are old enough to make some of their own decisions. They also are old enough to take on the consequences of the decisions they make. How they make their own decisions and how they handle the consequences of those decisions give us the information we need regarding how many of their decisions we need to make for them.

An example of good teen decision-making would be the decision to study instead of talk on the phone. A teen who says to his parents, "I'm not going to go to that party tonight. The children are going to be drinking, and I don't want to be a part of that," is making a good decision. A teen who comes home before curfew (not one minute but one hour early) and brings his friends with him is making good decisions. A teen who doesn't stamp out of the room yelling, "I hate you, I hate you, I hate you," when you say "no" is demonstrating some maturity. If your teen behaves maturely, you can give that teen a little more leeway than the teen who can't seem to stay on the right side of things. As parents we need to judge how maturely our teen behaves in other areas to help determine how maturely they are going to behave on the big issues of drinking, drug use and sexual activity. We have to know our child honestly—not who we want them to be but who they actually are.

Parental Instincts

They also want us to prevent them from getting into trouble. They believe we have parental instinct, and they want us to use it. While instinct is not always foolproof, by the time our children are in the sixth grade, we have all found ourselves in a situation in which, for some reason, we knew our child shouldn't do something—a party they were invited to, a movie they were going to see, a trip to the mall. Something in our heart told us they shouldn't do this. Many of the parents I meet ignore this instinct. It is common for a parent to tell me, "I know I shouldn't let her do this but. . . ." The "buts" can be endless. We all can think of reasons why we should give in against our better judgment, but if we feel we shouldn't let our child do something, it is our responsibility NOT to let him do it. Once we give in against our own best judgment (maybe we didn't want a fight, or we were tired, or we didn't have the whole story when we said "yes"—there are a million rationalizations for not doing our job), we put our teen in charge, just where he is not yet ready to be.

How do we reverse this once we have given our child control? It is very hard, and usually it results in some disagreements. But it is worth the effort. The sooner our child knows we are the "benevolent dictator," not a democratic leader, the easier it is to avoid those power struggles. If our child is accustomed to having power, she is going to fight us for more. If our child is accustomed to the hierarchy of the family, the more likely she is to listen and obey. If you are planning on changing your approach, be prepared for some arguments, plan your strategy and stick with your decisions. Remain calm, do not become engaged in the power struggle, say what your mean and mean what you say. Be up front with her, explaining that you were wrong: "We have learned some new things, and we will be changing our parenting." Wait three months. That is how long a change like this will take. (It feels like forever, but it isn't.)

Our children want us to trust our instincts, and they want to argue with us on it. They want us to say "no" to them. They want to give us an argument and still have us not change our mind. They want to tell you that you are the only parent who says "no," that this situation is the most socially embarrassing of their lives (it probably is), but you still shouldn't change your mind. When our middle school child tells us, "Everyone else can do this," he does not necessarily want us to change our mind so much as he wants us to get the other children's parents to provide more limits for their own children as well.

Discipline, Defined & Instilled

Discipline and punishment are not the same thing. Punishment may become necessary when discipline fails and naturally occurring consequences are not experienced adequately. Consequences are enforced when boundaries are crossed; the consequences should be reflective of the boundary. Actually, the more effective your discipline, the less punishment you will need to enact. One dad gave me an excellent analogy on discipline. Parents are the guard rails on a curvy road with no speed limit. Sometimes the traffic is going really fast, and sometimes the drivers lose their way. The guard rails keep them on the road, going in the proper direction. This is our job as parents: to keep our children on their road, moving in the right direction. Discipline will do this.

Discipline is the decision to get out of bed when the alarm goes off. Discipline is knowing the consequences before you perform the action. Discipline is structure and form. Going to school on time, coming home from school, going to practice, doing your homework, going to bed at a decent hour are all a part of this structure in discipline. This doesn't have to translate into a rigid life without any room for spontaneity. It is simply a matter of making sure that what has to be done gets done—that our responsibilities to our families, community and ourselves are fulfilled. No requirements for behavior, total freedom to choose what they want and when they want it, TV-watching when homework should be done, coming home at any time they please, not having work done for school because of talking on the phone—all of this shows a lack of discipline and structure. Learning to fulfill responsibilities to self (with schoolwork), to family (parents' worrying when their teen is out driving around) and others (monopolizing your friend's time when he should be doing his homework also) is crucial.

Discipline makes disciples. (In fact, the words "discipline" and "disciple" come from the same root word in English.) Let's think about Jesus' disciples for a minute. They were obedient (most of the time) even when they didn't understand why Christ was asking them to do certain things. They knew whom they were following even when they didn't have a clear understanding of why. Christ role-modeled discipline for us. He was kind but firm. (He clearly told the woman at the well to "sin no more.") He had expectations that he kept high for His followers, even when they didn't meet those expectations (the disciples' sleeping in the garden before His betrayal). He demonstrated just anger (the moneychangers in the temple). And He prayed to His Father to help Him do his job non-stop.

We as a modern generation of parents frequently feel compelled to justify our decisions to our children rather than to allow our decision just to stand. This habit easily opens the doors for controversy rather then communication. This is not a godly habit. The controversy demonstrates our child's unhappiness to us, and the unhappiness makes us doubt our choices. ("If my child is unhappy, I must be wrong.") The doubt opens the door for us to change our mind. This process does not demonstrate to our children the strength of whom they are supposed to be following; it demonstrates our own doubts about our leadership. It is difficult to follow a leader who is unsure of where he is taking you.

One way to prevent this power struggle is to take your time with decisions about what your child may or may not do. Think through the situation, and ask questions: "Who will be there?" "How long will you be there?" "Is an adult going to be with you?" "When will you be home?" "How are you getting home?" Say "yes" only when you are satisfied with the answers. Many teens ask permission when their parent is distracted. They tell mom or dad that they need the answer right now. Everything seems like an emergency. Do not respond under this kind of duress. You are likely to make a decision you will wish you hadn't. Be sure your child knows that you will take your time with decisions; if she can't give you the time to think it through, your answer has to be "no." I recommend that you expect your child to make her requests and answer your questions respectfully as well.

As adults, we have the capacity to take the long view; however, as teenagers, our children have the capacity to understand the moment. We must let our long view dictate our decisions. Who do we believe our child can be? What do we have to do to help her get there? When we look at the big picture, it is easy to become the leader our child needs to be able to follow. We become able to say, "I'm sorry that you are unhappy about this. I probably would be, too, if I were you; but as the parent, I have to make decisions based on what I know is right for your whole life, not just for today."

Discipline recognizes temptation and desire and puts guides in place to make it easier for our children to make the right decision. For example, if we know our teenager and a boyfriend or girlfriend will be tempted to become physically intimate if we leave them alone, we must avoid leaving them alone as much as possible. We have a "no girl/boyfriend in the house when no one is home" rule, we have a "no girl/boyfriend in your bedroom rule," and we have a "no overnight trips with your girl/boyfriend" rule.

Discipline means our children will become self-disciplined because they have experienced external discipline. Discipline will help our children to practice obedience. They learn to obey God by obeying their parents. Discipline means we will not have to "pick our battles." I do not believe in this form of child-rearing. Most of the time, when someone tells me, "I pick my battles," she has just told me a story in which she did not do what she believed was right for her child. "I can't stand that my child goes out of our house dressed that way, but I pick my battles"; "I don't want my child to watch that R-rated movie when she is fourteen, but I pick my battles." I do NOT endorse the "pick your battles" school of parenting. When you make that choice, you are saying that you are willing to "battle" your child. If you express your parental authority, you are going to have to fight with your child. This is an undesirable expectation that your child will fulfill every time you say "no." If you are expecting a battle, your child will be happy to give you one. That will never get you anywhere but in trouble that is hard to get out of. This is where power struggles are born. I believe that parents have to be very clear about what is right or wrong for their child and choose what is right. It is never necessary to have a fight with your child about it. YOU ARE THE PARENT, and what you say goes whether your child likes it or not. If your child wants to battle you, make him battle alone: "I'm sorry, but I'm not going to have a fight with you about this. I have made the decision that I believe is right. If you are going to fight with me, you will fight alone. I will not get involved in this with you." We will decrease the likelihood of battles because consequences are known beforehand. If the parents are known to be consistent in enforcing consequences, and children know which actions will enact consequences, it makes it much easier to coexist.

For example, our son Steve has his own car. He goes to school in another town, and he works even further away. So we viewed having his own transportation as a necessity. He loves the independence it gives him getting back and forth to school, work, and his other activities. We told him that if he ever gets a speeding ticket, we will sell his car, and he will lose that independence. We view speeding as a life-and-death choice for our son, and we know that teenage boys are high-risk for speeding. We had to choose a consequence that made clear our desire that our son not speed. He has to trust that we will enforce this consequence. He has learned over his lifetime that what we say we will do, we will do. His safety and well-being are important enough to us to construct a consequence that will be unforgettable. He knows that if he speeds, he loses his car. So far, so good. He does not want to lose this privilege.

How did Steve learn that we take our consequences seriously? By the small consequences we have enforced over the course of his lifetime. When we have to help our children learn their limits, we ask them, "What can we do so that this will never happen again?" And we give them some time to think it over. They usually come up with some pretty good ideas, and we enforce them. When I was writing this chapter, I had a hard time coming up with "punishments" that we had enforced over the years (our children are now 18 and 13), so at the dinner table I asked them about memorable punishments. None of us could think of any since the children were really small. Maggie remembered that I put all her dolls away once for a month when she was 8 or 9, and Steve remembered that I once told him, "I love you, honey. You are my son, and I'll always love you. But I don't like your behavior very much right now." They both seemed to think that this was enough to teach them we meant business so as not to push the limits beyond what our family found acceptable.

Discipline means we will experience increased peace in our households because everyone knows the rules and the consequences. And the children trust the consequences to be enacted if the rule is broken. If consequences are irregularly experienced, our children will try to avoid the consequences. They will push the envelope further and further, and they will keep coming back to us to try to wear us down. We will never have peace, and we will not have a teenager who trusts that we are in control for them.

Discipline Do's and Don'ts

Discipline is learned best from parents who have acquired self-discipline. "Do as I do" still works much better than "do as I say." Remember the story at the beginning of the chapter? What went wrong there? The parents made several discipline mistakes:

(1) Adequate party prevention was not practiced.

The parents should have talked to the neighbors and let them know they were going to be away for an overnight and asked them to keep an eye on the children and the house. They then should have said to the children, "You know that we are going to be away overnight this weekend, so we told Mr. and Mrs. So-and-So to keep an eye on things while we are gone. We feel much safer knowing they will be able to contact us if they have any concerns, so please feel free to let them know if you need anything."

(2) They did not allow the parents of children involved in their party to know what their children were up to and, consequently, to take corrective action themselves.

These parents did not call the parents of the other children, so the other parents continued to be ignorant of their own teens' high-risk behaviors and, therefore, were unable to take corrective action for their own child.

(3) They didn't allow their daughter to experience a consequence that would prevent her from doing this again.

They chose to ground their daughter for one month, but—and this is a big but—here they were one week later, waiting for her to show up at the football game in the family car!! And they were worried because she was late, and they had a big fight before she left the house! If she was grounded for a month, why did she go out with her friends only one week later?! Why did she have the family car to go out in?! By allowing her out when she was grounded, they demonstrated to her that they did not take her offense seriously.

(4) A bigger deal should have been made about the risk she put her entire family in just to have a party.

Remember that she was responsible for her younger siblings. What type of role-modeling did she and her parents provide for the younger children? Her family could have lost their home if one of the drinking and driving children had gotten into an accident, not to mention the emotional agony the entire family would live with.

(5) Grounding is rarely an effective form of discipline.

When we ground our child, we also ground ourselves, particularly if we have a child who is driving. Also, if we go out, no one is home to supervise the grounded teen. The begging and pleading or silent treatment that our child gives us while he is grounded wears us down, and we are likely to give in before the full time has elapsed. The teens I see tell me this is true, that this reluctance to keep them grounded makes grounding a very ineffective choice.

What could the parents of the other children have done?

(1) Call the house where their child is going to be that night and inquire about the party.

"Hi! This is Mary Ronan. I understand you're going to have a party tonight, and I was wondering if there is anything I can send along for you. Do you need any extra soda or chips?" We need to do this even (maybe mostly) for high school students. If our children are unwilling to tell us where they are going, we shouldn't allow them to go. One mom told me that her rule for her son is that if she can't go into the party and say "hi" to the parents, he can't go to the party. He understands the rule and doesn't even ask to go to parties his mom can't go into.

(2) Have a parent network in which we as parents are in the habit of talking to each other before our children are going out together at night.

If we start this habit when our children are young—fourth or fifth grade—our children expect it of us even as they become more independent. We don't have to become best friends with the parents of their friends, but we should be friendly enough to talk to them.

(3) We need to worry less about our child's popularity and more about their behaviors.

Popularity is fleeting: it counts most during middle and high school. I meet many parents who truly worry about how their parental decisions affect their child's popularity or how their child fits in. This concern interferes with the parent's ability to have effective discipline for their children. It is also short-term thinking when our children need us to be thinking long-term. We need to help our children see the big picture as we, at the same time, understand and have empathy for how difficult that is for a teen.

Some Tips on Consequences

Consequences help to increase self-discipline. They are enforced as external discipline when our child breaks a rule, either spoken or implied.

(1) They should fit the "crime" as closely as possible.

For example, if your child breaks curfew, he needs to stay home until you know you can trust him to come in on time again. When he can go back out again, the curfew needs to be changed to an earlier time. When he arrives home at the earlier time consistently, the curfew may be moved gradually to a later time. We are trying to teach responsibility and self-control, not just making our child suffer; but sometimes suffering has to occur to learn responsibility and self control.

(2) They do not have to be immediate.

Sometimes we aren't sure what we should do when our child is rebellious or disobedient. The worst time to think up a consequence is when we are mad. We are likely to state a consequence we can't easily enforce–"You're grounded for a month"–instead of thinking through the best consequence for the action. Take your time. Let your child know you are thinking about what to do, and you'll get back to them when you know.

(3) Your child can help you choose consequences.

Ask your child, "What should I do to be sure you remember never to let this happen again?" Give her a little time, 24 hours or so, to think of an appropriate consequence. They usually are tougher on themselves than we are on them. If we don't think the consequence is appropriate, we have a door open to discuss what makes a good consequence and what doesn't, finding a consequence that will work for all involved.

(4) Don't interfere with someone else's enforcement of a consequence on your child.

. If the school calls, support them. Don't try to get your child out of detention to attend sports practice. If the coach benches your son or daughter, support the coach. Be careful not to interfere with the authority another adult has over your child. We have to learn how to respond to all authority. Haven't we all had to do something that seemed unfair?

(5) Corrective action and anger usually aren't the best combination for lesson learning.

It is usually best to apply correction with a cool head. Our children should know we are unhappy, even angry, but shouting, yelling and swearing will cause them to remember the anger, not the correction. We want them to remember the correction and to know we are correcting them because we love them and that we see their potential and hope for the best for their future.

(6) Consequences can change.

If you explain a corrective action you have in mind and your child throws a fit, you can change your mind. Perhaps, you may need to intensify the consequences. A child can demonstrate poor self-control with these kinds of stamping-off-to-the-room, door-slamming events. You need to know that our child learned how and has the ability to have strong feelings and not act inappropriately on them.

Desire is a strong feeling. Do we want our children to give in and become sexually active? Peer pressure is a very strong feeling that can push children towards alcohol or drugs. We must take steps to help them develop the ability to control their response when strong feelings are present. The best time to do this is when we say "no" or when we correct them. We will know that our children are maturing when yelling, stomping and saying hurtful things are no longer their ways of dealing with anger. Their self-control then will be an asset as they face larger issues outside the home.

Some Tips on Discipline

(1) Discipline is a skill; it takes time to develop.

Be patient. God isn't finished with any of us yet. We are works in progress until we die. That gives us all plenty of time to get it right.

(2) Participation in activities that require discipline makes a difference.

Playing an instrument, writing a journal, observing nature, learning to sing, writing poetry or short stories, keeping a collection, and participation in the performing arts are all examples of activities that require discipline.

(3) Delayed gratification is necessary for self-discipline.

Help your child to learn to wait for what they want. $150.00 sneakers? Save up. Waiting to drive, waiting for the first date, waiting for independence—we all need to learn how to wait. Talk to your child about this. How would she feel if you spent all the family money on what you wanted and did not leave any aside for her? How would she like it if what you wanted was to be independent one day, so you left her? What would she think if you, as a parent, always put your own desires first? Learning to wait, to be long-term, is a long, uneasy process that needs to be enforced externally before it is realized internally. The only way our child will learn to live with delayed gratification is for us to live it by our example.

(4) Household responsibilities help to develop discipline.

Be sure your child is responsible for some of the work of the household. Who takes out the garbage, cleans the bathrooms, sets the table, cleans up the kitchen, vacuums, and does the laundry in your house? I hope it is not the parents. Children should have chores that make a difference in the running of the household. They should be taught how to do a task and then be expected to do it on their own. Our children take care of our pets, take care of the garbage, set the table and clean the kitchen. (My husband and I really like this one. We can sit and talk at the table after dinner while the children clean up. This is usually a pretty fun time in our house.) They clean their rooms once a week and do any other chores we need their help with on the weekends. When the work gets spread around among four people, the household is much easier to manage, and the parents are much happier— everyone wins. Besides, someday they are going to have households of their own, and they need to know how to do all of this. John Rosemund has some great ideas on how to structure household tasks in his book, *The Six-Point Plan for Raising Happy, Healthy Children.*

Discipline makes life easier, more peaceful, and simpler. We all feel better about ourselves when we know what the limits are and what the consequences will be when the limits are exceeded. Teenagers know they are not in control, and deep down they do appreciate having parents that provide the security of discipline for them. This is one of those jobs of child-rearing that the children appreciate later, maybe when they are parents themselves.

If developing responsible, God-fearing, self-disciplined members of the community is our goal in child-rearing, these are skills that take a lifetime to develop. While schools, extracurricular activities, church and the community can all support our efforts to help our child mature to adulthood, the ultimate responsibility is ours.

Things to Think About

- What type of discipline do you use most commonly?
- Do your children believe you when you set up limits and controls?
- Do you ever say you are going to enact a consequence and then not enact it or enact it to a lesser degree?
- Do you ever worry that you are too permissive?
- Do you relent when your child becomes upset?
- Do you view discipline as a long-term plan, or do you decide at the moment what is or is not acceptable?

Things to Do

- Pray about discipline in your household. Let God know the challenges you face, as well as what your weaknesses and strengths are regarding discipline, punishment and role-modeling.
- Set clear guidelines for behaviors. Let your child know what is truly unacceptable behavior. Will you allow drinking, drug use, sexual activity? How important is your curfew?
- Be consistent with the consequences. If you say you are going to do something, DO IT!! Don't say, "You're grounded for two weeks," if you are going to let them go out on Friday night.
- Don't yell. Modulate your voice even if it requires enormous self-control. Yelling demonstrates a loss of control and a loss of authority.

- Talk to your children about what is important to your family.
- Talk in general terms about your feelings about drugs, alcohol and sex before your child enters high school. TV shows and movies can provide a good starting point.
- Expect obedience, but remember that you won't always get it. Even Scripture tells us to "train up a child in the way he should go, and when he is old, he will not turn from it" (Proverbs 22:6).
- Don't despair if you make a mistake; we are all human. Sometimes we might be too strict, sometimes we might be too lenient; but aim for consistency, correcting any errors as you go along: "I'm sorry I said you could go tonight, but I did not know all the implications; and now that I know, I have to change my mind."

Scripture to Remember

- Hebrews 12:11 - No chastening seems joyful for the present, but painful; nevertheless, afterward it yields the peaceable fruit of righteousness to those who have been trained by it.
- Proverbs 29:15 - The rod and rebuke give wisdom, but a child left to himself brings shame to his mother.
- Proverbs 13:24 (NIV) - He who spares the rod hates his son, but he who loves him is careful to discipline him.
- Proverbs 19:18 - Chasten your son while there is hope, and do not set your heart on his destruction.
- 1 Thessalonians 5:14 - Warn those who are unruly, comfort the fainthearted, uphold the weak, be patient with all.
- Proverbs 13:18 (NIV) - He who ignores discipline comes to poverty and shame, but whoever heeds correction is honored.
- James 5:20 - Let him know that he who turns a sinner from the error of his way will save a soul from death and cover a multitude of sins. (WOW!!!)

Alcohol is a gateway drug: once a teen starts drinking, he is more likely to progress to other harder substances such as marijuana, "huffing" or inhaling common household products (glue, correction fluid, freon, paint fumes), ecstasy, hallucinogens such as LSD, and cocaine and crack. Teens tend to "add" drugs rather than abandon one drug in favor of another; therefore, it is easy for a teen to become a multiple drug abuser.

4

DRINKING & Drug Abuse

My husband and I were at a party in which we didn't know any-one but the hosts. We were sitting with adults from several towns talking about our teenagers and what they were up to. You know the conversation; you've probably had it yourself. Two parents were talking about their teenage sons and all of their social activities. These parents were actually bragging about the popularity of their children and how socially active they were. This led into a competi-tion between the parents about how "understanding" they were of their children's social needs. These parents wanted to be "cool" par-ents, so they proceeded to tell us about the most recent parties they threw for their sons. One father proudly told us how they had such a great party that the "cops" even came to break it up! This is the same guy who said he had a swimming pool installed and asked us if we had ever heard of the word "nubile"!! (How would you like your daughter to be at one of this man's parties?) Another mother felt free to express her disgust with the "uptight" parents (like my husband and me) who would not want her serving their underaged child alcohol. "Why should I feel responsible if some uptight parent doesn't want their child to drink?"

I'm going to give you a little hint about something in high school that gets more kids into trouble than anything else: parties at each other's houses. That's the number one high-risk social activity for children. In a study by the Drug

Abuse Resistance Education (DARE) program in North Carolina, tracking more than 10,000 students over a four-year period, it was found that 18% of eighth graders and 24% of ninth graders reported drinking alcohol more than ten times or being drunk at least once in the previous thirty days.[1]

In many of the communities where I work, underage drinking is not as unacceptable to the parents as it should be. I would imagine that there are adults in your town—particularly if your town is wealthy—who allow drinking at parties at their houses or who even provide alcohol to teens at parties. The parents understand that there is alcohol consumption, so they take the car keys and invite boys and girls to sleep over if they are too drunk to drive and mistakenly believe they are doing something responsible for your child.

These parents felt that it was within their rights not just to allow but actually to encourage your child or mine to break the law. What does this choice do to your careful plan of teaching delayed gratification and self-control? I only can imagine the confusion a teenager must feel when an adult encourages him to break not only his parents' rules and regulations but the laws of his community as well.

This is one of the areas in which it is easy for the children to find themselves in over their heads. Distinct boundaries with clearly outlined consequences, along with practice at delayed gratification and self-control, can make it much easier for our teens to make a healthy decision in this situation. Once drinking is taking place, there is not another good decision that takes place. Children don't drink because they like the taste. They drink to get drunk. How can we expect our child to be able to have sober fun in college or as an adult if they never practice sober fun as a teenager?

My own surveys of more than 20,000 students in eighth through twelfth grades confirm drinking as a very common secret children keep from their parents. While approximately 25% of eighth graders in my survey are drinking, that number skyrockets to nearly 50% during ninth grade and 70% by their junior year. This is corroborated by a large study published in *Addiction* magazine, which found that 90% of high school students have tried alcohol, more than 50% of high school students currently use alcohol, and more than 28% of high school students binge-drink. (Binge-drinking is defined as more than five drinks in a row during the two weeks before the study.[2]) The year of greatest risk to begin drinking appears to be between the freshman and sophomore years of high school. This is true of all high-risk behaviors, so freshman year requires great parental vigilance on this issue as well as on the others we will discuss later.

Alcohol is not the only substance that brings children to places where they find themselves in trouble because they are not thinking clearly, driving safely or choosing wisely. Other popular substances today are very easy to gain access to in any high school and many middle schools throughout the United States. A friend of mine about to undergo surgery for breast cancer had her two teenage sons tell her that if she needed marijuana when she started chemotherapy, they knew whom to buy it from! These boys are students in a small, suburban, Christian, college prep high school. They told their mom they would have "no problem" getting her what she needed! (The most recent data for marijuana smoking, from a 1997 study done by the Partnership for a Drug-Free America, showed dramatic increases in the use of marijuana in middle school students. 8% of sixth grade, 23% of seventh grade and 33% of eighth grade students admitted to having used marijuana.[3])

Alcohol is a gateway drug: once a teen starts drinking, she is more likely to progress to other harder substances such as marijuana, "huffing" or inhaling common household products (glue, correction fluid, freon, paint fumes), ecstasy, hallucinogens such as LSD, and cocaine and crack. Teens tend to "add" drugs rather than abandon one drug in favor of another; therefore, it is easy for a teen to become a multiple drug abuser.

According to Dr. Meg Meeker, the following are the most common risk factors for using drugs:

- parent or relative who is a substance abuser
- poor self-esteem
- family instability (divorce or severe dysfunction)
- low achievement (especially in school)
- aggressive personality (ADHD creates higher risk)
- history of sexual or physical abuse
- psychological disorders, especially depression.[4]

When the children tell me their parents ought to know and prevent them from getting into trouble, I take them seriously. One way to help is to be very careful about the parties they go to. The most effective way to screen parties is to call the house when we hear there is a party. "I hear there is a party tonight. Can I send anything along? Soda? Chips?" If someone is having a bunch of teenagers, they are going to need soda and food. That's a friendly way to open the conversation.

Once the parents confirm that there is going to be a party, the first thing you want to be sure of is that there will be adequate supervision. Find out exactly how they plan to supervise the party and ask if alcohol will be in the home. If they say they are going to be home, you will want to know how often they are going to be in the same room as the children. I never used to suggest this, but I've had several parents who had given a party tell me they didn't even realize the children were drinking until 10:30 at night, when their own child was slurring words. Then they realized drinking was taking place. These were parents who were sending the little sister down to circulate snacks and drinks. Yet their own child was drinking. When the parents are in the bedroom on the third floor and the children are in the basement, that is not a supervised party. We need to know how many adults are going to be there. Offer to help out as extra chaperones. This isn't going to make you popular with your children, but it will help your children stay safe.

This is when parents' hearts are tugged in many directions. The fact is that a non-drinking teen will have fewer social outlets than a drinking teen. Alcohol abuse is so ingrained into our teen culture that a non-drinking teen will have a different experience throughout high school and college from that of a drinking teen. Here's an example. Over the summer before my son's senior year of high school, we attended a party with families we are very close to who have sons and daughters my son's age and older, already in college. When we arrived at the party, the children were all sitting together talking in one room, and the adults were close by in another room, constantly walking past the children with food and sodas. My son came in and sat behind the table full of teens, first just listening in on their conversation, about to sit down and join them. In very short order, he was in the room with the adults, joining in our conversation. Without asking him, I knew why. These young men and women were talking about one thing: drinking. They were talking about their fake ID's, big drinking parties and picking up guys and girls. My son had nothing to contribute to the conversation. He does not drink. And he was uncomfortable listening to all the "gross" talk (about girls and what they'll do).

Is my son a "goody-goody"? He doesn't view himself that way. He views himself as long-term, moving forward towards his future without creating complications now. But the complications he has now are the limits of his social life in an alcohol-oriented teen world. Are the other boys "bad" boys? They don't view themselves that way, nor do their parents, but they certainly are making harmful choices for themselves in the short term. It is the worry about popularity that causes so many parents to make mistakes with their child about drinking. It was the worry about popularity that made the parents at the beginning of this chapter believe their children were making acceptable choices in drinking.

Last year I was speaking with parents at a high school in a small New England town. As the evening was getting started, several teens came in and sat in the classroom where my presentation was taking place. Even though this night was not meant for teens' participation, I really couldn't gracefully ask them to leave. So I just went forward with my parents' night program. When we started to discuss the problem of drinking and parties, these children became very resistant to my message. They worried about the popularity of teens whose parents don't let them drink. They believed that parents who over-supervised in high school would caused their children to go off the deep end with drinking once they got to. They said if their parents didn't let them drink, they simply would lie to them and tell them they were going to someone else's house and then go to the forbidden party and drink anyway.

As we spoke, I addressed their concerns: statistics show that (1) you are more likely to binge-drink (five or more drinks at a time) in college if you binge-drink in high school, (2) you are more likely to develop a drinking problem if you begin drinking while you are underage, and (3) you are more likely to become sexually active if you are drinking.

We talked about the role of popularity in parents' concerns (not overriding). Because not drinking does alter a high school student's social life, it actually can be a very isolating decision. We parents need to remember to keep the long view for our child. Drinking can lead to devastating life-changing consequences. Anything from a drinking and driving accident to date rape to a lifetime fighting addictions is possible once teens begin to drink. These factors must be considered when we are tempted to make popularity a high priority.

When the evening ended, the teens stayed around while I talked with some parents and packed up. I thought they were probably upset with me and wanted to continue our discussion, so I was a little nervous. After everyone left, the young men and women introduced themselves to me. These juniors and seniors in high school attended to meet a continuing education requirement for their job in daycare. (They really did not want to be there.)

This is what they said: "Everything you said about drinking and parties is true. We were mad at first because you were blowing our cover, and that made us feel uncomfortable. But we want to tell you to keep up the good work. Parents need to know this stuff." One of these boys already had run into alcohol trouble and will never be able to have even a casual drink of wine at dinner, and he isn't legal drinking age yet!

When your children are small and are going to other people's houses, that's the time to start making those phone calls. Get in the habit so your child is used to your calling. If you have fourth, fifth or sixth graders, start making those calls even if you know there is going to be an adult there. You can begin making the calls during high school, but you should expect more resistance than if you start at a younger age. You should still make the calls, it's just a little more difficult. I'll give you something to ask about for those parties, too. Inquire which movie, if any, will be showing, but we'll talk about that in chapter 9 on popular culture. It's the habit that counts. Your children can learn to depend on you to help them avoid situations they are not yet prepared to handle.

The good news in all of this is that parents do make a difference. The main protective factors, identified through research, that will help your teen avoid the dangers of drug and alcohol use are closely related to the way we raise our children. Teens do best when they experience the following:

- family connectedness
- school connectedness
- religion and prayer as important to their lives
- high levels of self-respect.[5]

And in the following areas, parental involvement in school and home will have a positive impact on the choices our children make throughout their teen years:

- knowing who our children are with and what they are doing
- taking our children with us when we worship and inviting them into a relationship with God through prayer and observance of the rituals of our faith,
- the opportunity to be involved in activities and experiences that encourage self-respect.

We can understand the value of the time and resources we spend with our children when we have the tangible results of a substance-free teen.

Things to Think About

- What are your opinions on underage drinking and drug use?
- Do you know parents you can network with regarding the issues of parties and drinking?
- Have you ever talked with your child about drinking and drug use and the consequences?
- Have you talked about the consequences of not drinking and how to handle them? (See chapter 5 on pressure for ideas.)
- What kind of role model are you with respect to alcohol consumption? Are you sober? Do your children see you have fun without drinking?

Things to Do

- Pray for your child about the issue of alcohol and drugs. Remember, God is with them even when we are not, and He loves your child even more than you do (as hard as that is to believe).
- Talk to your child about drinking. Talk about what she can do if she is ever at a party in which drinking is taking place. Hint: Tell them you will rescue them. All she has to do is call you up, and you will come and get her.

She can step outside, and no one will have to know that it is you that will be picking her up.

- Establish VERY CLEAR boundaries on alcohol and other drug use. Be sure your child understands the consequences of drinking underage or using other substances. Be even more sure you enact those consequences if you become aware of any substance use. (See chapter 3 on discipline.)
- Talk to your child about how not to drink at a party.
- Call every household where your child will be attending a party.
- If you drive your child to a party, go into the home and say "hello" to the parents. Check on pick up time.
- Role-model appropriate alcohol use. Don't drink and drive. Stay sober.

Scripture to Remember

- 1 Peter 5:8 - Be sober, be vigilant; because your adversary the devil walks about like a roaring lion, seeking whom he may devour.
- 1 Corinthians 5:11 - [Do] not . . . keep company with anyone . . . who is sexually immoral, or covetous, or an idolater, or a reviler, or a drunkard, or an extortioner— [do] not even . . . eat with such a person.
- Romans 12:1 - Present your bodies a living sacrifice, holy, acceptable to God.
- Romans 12:21 - Do not be overcome by evil, but overcome evil with good.
- 1 Thessalonians 5:21 (NIV) - Test everything. Hold on to the good.
- 1 Peter 1:13 (NIV) - Therefore, prepare your minds for action; be self-controlled; set your hope fully on the grace to be given you through Jesus Christ.

Recognize the peer pressure you feel from other parents. Have you had the thought, "Maybe I am too strict about this issue"? Have you ever felt like the "only one" when you've made a decision for your child? Do you worry about the effects your decisions have on your child's social life? Have you ever thought, "Everyone else seems to think this is okay"? You have experienced parental peer pressure.

5

PRESSURE, a Powerful Foe

When I work with seventh graders, I have them solve problems based on the Ten Commandments. They act out skits in which they have to solve a contemporary moral dilemma, like being asked to drink at a party or going to a movie their parents would not approve of. Seventh graders reveal themselves by imagining pressure coming from someone they don't like. They never imagine pressure to come from someone they like, even though that's most likely where it's going to come from. When seventh graders act out pressure to drink, they act as though the pressure is going to be overt and somewhat hostile: "Drink this beer or we'll think you're a jerk." They also act out their responses to be corrective: "Drinking is against the law, and my parents wouldn't approve. You shouldn't drink either."

When I ask my students to list the three biggest problems facing teens today, the third most common answer is pressure, preceded only by sex and drugs/alcohol. But the pressure is the reason many of our children get involved in drugs, alcohol or sexual activity in the first place. Our children experience pressure from a wide variety of sources: friends, school, family, culture. They have difficulty anticipating what pressure is going to feel like and realistically evaluating how they will respond in a situation in which the pressure feels overwhelming.

Under "Friendly" Fire

The truth is that the pressure is very friendly. Most children by ninth grade will walk into a party where some friends are already present with drinks in their hands, laughing, talking, having fun, being with their friends; and someone will say, "Hey, want one?" This is the moment of pressure. Every child with a drink in his hand has, at some point, gone through the thought process, "If I don't drink, will they think I'm a 'goody-goody'? Will I get into trouble with my parents if I say "yes"? Will everyone think I'm a wimp if I say 'no'?" This dialogue goes on in our children's brains; but because they don't know what to say, they say, "Sure." It is the easiest thing to say.

Our children, like us, don't care what someone they don't like thinks of them. They care what the children they *like* think. If your child's friends don't drink, it is easy for your child to turn his back on drinking. But if your child's friends are drinking, that's a different story. It is hard to turn your back on your circle of friends. The *first* thing we need to clear up for them is that pressure to drink, use drugs and be sexually active doesn't come from strangers. You are not pressured by strangers to drink; your friends are drinking. You are not pressured by strangers to have sex; your boyfriend or girlfriend (along with your best friends if you are a boy) pressure you to have sex. You are not pressured by strangers to smoke pot; your friends invite you to do it.

In a survey done by *Parade Magazine*, 83% of teenage girls (ages 12-19) stated that girls participated in sex because boys pressured them or they fear their boyfriends will drop them if they don't. Eighty-six percent of teens thought the boys pressured each other to have sex. The girls reported that many girls become sexually active to be popular and to feel loved and wanted.[1] This is pressure at its worst. It is experienced by these young girls (and boys) as an internal pressure to comply with the norms of their culture, both the general popular culture and the culture of their friends.

The *second* thing that is helpful for our children to understand is how much of the pressure is internal. We want to do things we know we shouldn't do. Our children are going to want to have sex, have a drink with their friends, go someplace we don't want them to go, watch a movie they aren't yet ready to see. Temptation is a human condition. We can help them recognize the internal pressure of temptation that makes the external (peer) pressure harder to fight. It is okay for us to tell our children they may want to do things they know are wrong for them. We also should let them know clearly that just wanting to do something does not make it right to do and that sometimes the internal pressure is hardest to fight. The wanting itself isn't the problem; it is the acting on the desire that gets us into trouble. I use the very simple analogy of the cookies in the pantry. I want one of those cookies. I could probably have one, and no one would know but me. If I eat the cookie, I relieve the pressure of wanting it, but I now add the feeling that I shouldn't have eaten it (guilt) and the good chance that I won't eat the healthy food at dinner because I have filled up on the unhealthy stuff. The pressure will go away if I ignore it; but once I've eaten the cookie, I can't undo my poor choice.

The *third* thing our children need to know is that much of their pressure comes from our popular culture. Watch almost any TV show, and you will find someone having sex outside of marriage. Most popular music has people who are acting on their feelings without thought for the consequences. Many video games encourage acting on every feeling you have no matter what the result is. You can read many contemporary magazines to find out how to give in to your desires, no matter what they are. Our teens have pressure to make harmful choices for themselves everywhere they turn. It is much harder to make good decisions with all that pressure from so many different sources.

Modeling Pressure Resistance

What can we do as parents? We need to recognize the challenge of pressure and understand that this pressure leads to temptation. Temptation can strengthen our children, increasing their resilience, improving self-respect, and building character. Or it can crush them, leading them down a road of self-destruction and harm to their family. The difference is in the preparation for the pressure experience. Most of us would probably want pressure to strengthen our child, polish her, bring out the best in her. We must show her how to resist pressure.

The first place we can role-model resistance to pressure is with our child, when we say "no" to a party, movie or other event our child wants to attend and our child pressures us to change our mind. If we as an adult can't resist pressure from a thirteen year old, how can we expect a thirteen year old to resist pressure? We know how tough pressure can be, especially if you have a child who follows you around the house everywhere you go, whining and pleading, "Oh, come on, can't I go?" "Why can't I do it? Everyone else can!" "Please, please, pleeeeeeease." That child is going to wear you out. *Don't let him*. You just say, "Your ability to persevere is going to take you far in life, but it's going to get you nowhere with me. I've made the right decision, and I'm obligated to make that right choice for you."

You have to show them how to resist the pressure, how to stick with it, even when the pressure is high. Say "no" nicely. Don't raise your voice. Don't make a big fight. Don't give in. If you think it's something your child ought not to be doing, it's something your child ought not to be doing. We need to show our children how to resist pressure from anyone: we role-model this by resisting pressure from them.

Parents also will experience pressure from other parents. This is another opportunity to demonstrate resistance. Don't be afraid to share your feelings with your children. Let them know that parental peer pressure makes it hard for you to make the decisions you need to make: "I'd love to have you go to that party—or, see that movie, go to the concert—and I understand other parents are allowing their children to go. But I have to make my decision based on what I know is right. I'm sorry to disappoint you."

Recognize the peer pressure you feel from other parents. Have you had the thought, "Maybe I am too strict about this issue"? Have you ever felt like the "only one" when you've made a decision for your child? Do you worry about the effects your decisions have on your child's social life? Have you ever thought, "Everyone else seems to think this is okay"? You have experienced parental peer pressure. How do you respond to this? Do you give in? If so, then you might want to evaluate your tools for handling the pressure that you feel. What does your child see when you change your mind as a result of pressure? How is your child learning to discern the correct response to pressure if she can't observe you responding appropriately?

Talk about the pressure they may feel as an adult for money, prestige, good grades in college, and a "big" job; and talk about the consequences of choosing to do wrong as an adult to relieve a little pressure. This pressure as a teenager is practice for all those decisions that have to be made as adults, so you will want them to practice the right response.

After speaking at a Catholic school, I received a call from a sixth-grade student who was researching peer pressure for her school science fair. She was doing a study to find out the age in which pressure first appears. Her results did not surprise her, but they did surprise me, though I spend all my time with teenagers. Most of the students in her research experienced pressure to do something they knew was wrong by fifth grade! Pressure started with something small, like giving your homework to a friend to copy, swearing, or going somewhere your parents wouldn't want you; but it grows to something much bigger with alcohol, drugs, and sex. (By the way, she won first place!)

Practicing Positive Resistance

This tells us to start our pressure prevention plan early. Our children need have a clear set of defined family values:

- They need to know our stand on the difference between right and wrong.
- They must experience consequences for their actions.
- They need to be able to talk to us about what is happening in their lives, have us listen, take them seriously and give practical, loving advice. We have to talk, talk, talk about pressure and how to handle it and listen, listen, listen to our child's concerns. See chapter 3 on discipline and chapter 6 (next) on talking and listening for more advice on effective communication.

In our house, we call situations in which we want to do one thing but "should" do something else a "character-building experience." This makes our children roll their eyes at us, but it also makes them roll up their sleeves and do the right thing. We can understand the difficulty of making a right decision, especially when we want to do the wrong thing and probably could get away with it or even rationalize it. But we still expect the right decision no matter what kind of pressure is felt. Our children can predict which situations we are going to define as character building, and we will often have a joke about it. This predictability benefits the children. It helps to "pressure-proof" them. Does it mean they will always do the right thing? Of course not. I don't always do the right thing. How can I expect my child to? But we want them to try. We want them to know what the right thing is and to be able to make their decisions (good and bad) on their own, not just as a result of pressure from their friends.

It is very helpful for our middle school children to practice their refusal skills. We can help them with this with friendly, supportive conversation. The younger our middle school child is, the more effective this practice will be. I recommend starting role-playing with your fifth or sixth grade child. Remember when your child was a kindergarten student or first grader? If he had trouble making friends, you gave him words he could use to make a friend. "Hi, my name is John. What is yours?" "Do you want to play this game with me?" We actually supplied words he could use. We want to continue to do this for our middle school child. Ask what she would do if her friend invited her over when there weren't going to be any parents home. You pretend you are the friend, and give your daughter a chance to think up what she could say in response: "No, I'd get in big trouble at home, but thanks anyway," or "Why don't you come over to my house, I have 'such and such' that we could do." Practice saying the words. You can do this in the car, at the dinner table or when you are watching TV together and you see someone make a poor choice: "What could you have said if you were in that situation?" Not only does it help our child to be able to plan, but it is also very beneficial not to have to think up a clever response when your young teen is feeling the incredible stress of peer pressure. Sometimes in our house we come up with really outrageous things to say that make us all laugh. This eases some of the anxiety about the pressure, but it also gives some pretty funny ideas at the same time.

Children find it very effective to relieve pressure with a joke or silly comment. We don't want them to take this so seriously that they are lecturing their friends about their behaviors all the time. It is a good idea if you have a very serious child to let him practice saying funny things. We want our child to be able to respond in a way that feels natural to them but also does not create a total outcast experience from the peer group.

Unhealthy Parental Pressure

Sometimes parents are the root of the pressure their teen experiences. If we try to live vicariously through our teen, it is easy to apply unrealistic pressure to perform. Our children need our encouragement to do their best. They need our expectations for acceptable and appropriate behavior, but there is a line between healthy and unhealthy pressure. If I want my child to perform to please me, not because of her own interest, I may be having unrealistic expectations. If I want my child to get all A's but she works very hard and diligently and gets B's, that pressure for the A's is not helpful but harmful. If I want my son to be the star of the football team but he would rather be the team manager, my pressure becomes unhealthy for him. We see this kind of pressure more and more in today's competitive social culture. Simply attend one soccer game for nine year olds, and you can see parental pressure in action.

We as parents must walk that fine line between encouragement and pressure. This requires some self-evaluation of the reasons we are applying this pressure to our child. Do we know for sure that our child is capable of what we are expecting but just needs a slight push to rise up to the expectations? Are we feeling competitive with other children or other parents and, therefore, are trying to "win" something over someone else? Is our child pursuing an activity that is pleasurable and stimulating for her, or is she doing an activity just to please me?

As a mother who has spent most of my children's growing up years carting them to performing arts activities, I regularly see the kind of pressure parents can apply to their children "for their own good." Activities like sports, dance, music, theatre, and student government are for the fun and development of our child, not to give the parents bragging rights. Such activities give children benefits such as a sense of themselves, a pleasurable hobby, practice in working with others, and a constructive way to spend their time. Discipline and self-control also will be developed. Parents can spoil this with competitive expectations that their child be "the best." If you have ever noticed this tendency in yourself, be aware.

This kind of pressure can be crushing for a child's sense of himself.

Things to Think About

- What issues give you parental peer pressure? What do you do about it?
- Are you able to resist pressure from your child? Could you begin to resist if you really tried?
- What types of pressure does your child experience? Friends? School? Family? Money? Fitting in?
- Have you talked with her about pressure? Could you?
- Do you pray about your child's pressures and his/her response?
- How much do you have invested in your child's activities? Grades at school? Sports? Music? Are you more invested than your child is? Is a disproportionate amount of family resources being used for one child's endeavors over the other children's?

Things to Do

- Pray about the pressure your child may be experiencing now and in the future. Be specific about the pressures you worry about the most: friends, drugs, school, boy/girlfriend, telling the truth.
- Talk to your child about pressure. Ask where they think pressure will come from. Role-play how to handle it. Give your child words to say in different pressure situations. Start these conversations early.
- Talk about right and wrong.
- Talk about family values—what is important to you as a family.
- Be clear about consequences.
- Demonstrate how to resist pressure. Talk about the pressures you experience and how you manage them.

Scripture to Remember

- 1 Corinthians 10:13 - No temptation has overtaken you except that which is common to man. God is faithful. He will not allow you to be tempted beyond what you are able, but with temptation will also make the way of escape so that you will be able to bear it.
- Proverbs 13:20 - He who walks with the wise grows wise, but a companion of fools will be destroyed.
- Proverbs 14:15 - A simple man believes anything, but a prudent man considers well his steps.
- Proverbs 15:23 (NIV) - A man finds joy in giving an apt reply—and how good is a timely word!
- Proverbs 16:7 - When a man's ways are pleasing to the Lord, He makes even his enemies to be at peace with him.

. . . Great news for us parents! Our children actually want us to talk to them about the issues that worry us the most. . . . The not-so-great news is that only 39% of children have parents that talk to them. The average teen spends only 7 minutes per day talking with her mom and 3 1/2 minutes per day talking with her dad! . . . They don't want us to lecture them. . . . They don't want us to do it in a way that feels like one-sided communication. They want us to listen to their thoughts, their ideas and their worries.

6

TALKING & Listening

In order to have talking time during the school year, the first choice I had to make was to turn off the telephone every afternoon from the time the children came home from school until the time I left for work. This turned out to be a great idea because it gave us all my afternoon to talk, to work out difficulties, to help with homework problems, and simply to be present in the house. It wasn't always great for my job, but it was consistently great for my family. I can honestly say our long after-school snacks and the talking time sitting at our kitchen counter are some of my favorite memories of my children's growing up years. These are also some of the happiest memories I have from my own growing up, my mom's sitting and talking to me at the kitchen table. We did a lot of high-risk prevention at that table. These are the conversations in which my mother prepared me to avoid premarital sexual activity!

Talking to your teenager is the number one preventative action you can take to help your children avoid trouble with sex, drugs, alcohol and pressure. This is according to the thousands of twelfth-grade students I've asked over the past ten years. In survey after survey, we are told that parents have the most influence over drug and alcohol use and sexual activity. This is great news for us parents! Our children actually want us to talk to them about the issues that worry us the most.

The "Silent Treatment"

The not-so-great news is that only 39% of children have parents that talk to them. The average teen spends only 7 minutes per day talking with her mom and 3 1/2 minutes per day talking with her dad![1] Not only are parent busy, but they are also worried about what to say and how to bring up sensitive subjects without saying the wrong thing. Say what is in your heart: "It is my greatest fear that you will harm yourself in some irreparable way." Bring these subjects up with sensitivity and honesty: "This is really difficult for me to talk about." Saying anything at all with love, compassion and your child's best interest at heart is saying the right thing. Teens have some ideas about what type of talking is most effective. They don't want us to lecture them; they don't want us to do it in a way that feels like one-sided communication. They want us to listen to their thoughts, their ideas and their worries.

Be a Storyteller

Sharing stories from our youth is a great way to connect to our children. Look for opportunities to share lessons you have learned from past mistakes without sharing too many details. Children don't want you to say, "Yes, I was promiscuous," or "I used drugs or got drunk every weekend." They don't imagine their parents as children. They imagine them to be the age they are now, so those aren't the stories they need to hear. You want to choose the stories in which you successfully combatted pressure. Choose stories about the troubles friends had and what lessons were learned through those troubles.

Choose your stories with an ear to your listener and the message you want your listener to have. We should never lie to our children, but there may be things in our past life that should be kept to ourselves. The lessons that we learned can be shared with our children without giving the details: "You know, I don't really want to give you permission to make the same mistakes I made. You have to make your own. So I'll let you know what I learned, but the details of the specific mistakes are best kept to myself." They know we are not perfect; they live with us! Yet they have a desire to learn from our experiences.

Every child doesn't ask questions about his parents' past, but some will. You probably know which child of yours will ask them. You also will be able to judge if your child is asking the question to someday use the information as justification for his own behaviors or if he is asking so he can make better decisions for himself.

Be an Advisor

They want us to tell them the dangers and risks of sex, drugs and alcohol. Our children appear very savvy and knowledgeable about these issues. They learn about them in school; but their information is very superficial, and they struggle with the right-and-wrong aspect of their decisions. Parents are the people responsible for filling in the blanks. We do not have to be experts about sex, drugs or alcohol. We just have to know what we believe. We need to express these beliefs very clearly to our children. If you are not sure where you stand on these subjects, please read the chapters covering these problems to help develop your opinion.

They want us to give them language to use in certain situations. (Refer to chapter 5 on pressure, particularly the story of the seventh graders' giving their friends a lecture on drinking, on page 65.) They say "yes" when under pressure because it's the easy thing to say. So we need to give them the words. We need to tell them they don't have to correct their friends' behavior. Their responsibility is to be sure that their own behavior matches up to their own family's standards.

The best thing to tell them to do when they feel under pressure is to make a joke; be funny, be light: "Someday when I run for president, I don't want you to use this against me." "No, thanks. I operate with few enough brain cells as it is." They need to find a response that is comfortable for them, that they can imagine themselves using with their friends. We can review those options with them.

Everyplace a Roundtable

Many parents try to cover their bases by planning one big "talk." It is much better to cover these topics through ongoing conversations in a variety of settings. The dinner table is an excellent place to include the whole family in planning ways to handle tough situations. Keep it casual and use your sense of humor to help your children prepare exactly what they will say or do. Then when pressure arises, they will be ready with a response.

Another good place to have difficult conversations is at bedtime. Every night say "goodnight" to your child in their bed. This is tough if you like to go to bed at nine and your children stay up until midnight. You're going to have to work that out somehow. But even with your big children, even with your high school students, it's okay to say, "It's time for bed." We can do that; it is part of our job. Tell them to head up. Give them a little time up in their room: quiet, no TV, only quiet music, reading, getting ready for the next day. Show up in their bedroom every night. The last words your child should hear from you is, "Honey I love you. You are the greatest, and I'm glad you are my child. You are dear to me." Your main purpose during these nighttime visits is to tell them you love them. That's your primary job. So, you're going to tell them that you love them, and you're going to ask them, "What can I pray for tonight?"

It is so important that your children hear these words not only from their mom but also from their dad. I really want to encourage you fathers to say these words not only to your daughters but also to your big 200-pound sons as well. Dad's loving influence counts not just during the challenging teen years but also throughout the rest of your child's life.

What happens with this nighttime conversation if it's not something you've done before? At first your older children are going to think you're a little crazy. They will wonder what is causing you to come up every night and say "I love you." By three months, it will break their hearts if you don't show up. (It takes three months to make the habit.) If your child is reluctant about this new habit at first, let him know you understand this to be a little different but that you will try it every night for three months. If they still don't like it after that, you'll stop. That's a fair deal. By three months they will say, "Are you coming up? I'm falling asleep."

The most consistent piece of feedback I receive on my program is that these bedtime goodnights open doors to conversations those families never knew they were going to have. Even when families are struggling terribly with conversation— they can't talk without having a fight—these nighttime "I love you's" can break down walls. And it's just a matter of our showing up, being sure they see at least one of us every night. I know it's hard in today's world to have both of us, but they should have at least one of us every single night.

Pray about these conversations daily. Ask the Lord to guide you in your words and touch. He will give you the words you need to discuss the topics most important to you and your child. More importantly, He will give you the courage to try.

The car is another excellent place to have conversations about sensitive issues. It is easier to talk about something difficult when you and your teen don't have to make eye contact. If you are anything like us, you spend plenty of time in the car together. One of the biggest differences I noticed when my son got his license was that now we had to carve out the time to talk that had occurred naturally when I was driving him around. This has been a challenge for us in our typically busy American household, especially because I work in the evening.

Evening work was always a great choice for us when our children were small. I was with them during the day, and my husband was with them in the evening. We were grateful to have the option of not having to use daycare. When our children started school, I had the freedom to volunteer in their schools and be an active part of their academic experience. When Stephen started high school in another town, my husband drove him every morning and I picked him up every afternoon and drove him to his lessons or his friend's. This assured lots of talking time—no radio, no distractions, no sister (who was in school until later in the day).

When he started driving himself to school, to lessons and to after-school activities, we lost a big piece of talking time. To make up the time, as mentioned at the beginning of the chapter, we created new opportunities to talk.

So now that the time is closing in on us and our son will be going off to college in one more year, we have chosen to do something radical. I've stopped going out to work, at least for my son's last year of high school. I know this sounds like a crazy choice, particularly when we are about to face the enormous tuition expenses of college. This seems like the time to work more and store up our financial resources. But the reality is that it's time to work less, much less. Our son may not be around all that much himself next year, and I want to be sure I'm around when he is. This is our last year of long, leisurely conversations, unfettered time with him, and regular family dinners. Stephen's leaving will be hard for Maggie also. However, this year will give her time to talk about, anticipate and prepare herself for the change our family is about to experience. Talking will be an important part of everyone's adjustment to our next phase of family life.

I encourage you to find time for regular, meaningful communication within your family. It may be during dinner, bedtime, carpooling, or some other time that works well for you. Make whatever changes are necessary to have enough opportunities for quality communication.

Honing Communication Skills

The ability to engage a listener, speak persuasively, and know when and how to bring up sensitive topics are skills we can help our child to develop. We need to learn how to disagree agreeably; parents can and should role-model this for their children. One excellent way for children to learn this is to see Mom and Dad work through disagreements in a productive manner. It is a good idea to have some parameters for how to talk to each other when you disagree. This is an area in which your child can develop self-control and learn how to behave in a more restrained way than they feel. I suggest a "no heat" rule. When you are in a disagreement and someone—it can be anyone involved—raises his voice, you separate: leave the room for some cooling off. Come back together and begin working toward resolution. If "heat" happens again, split up, come back later and try again. Keep at this until it becomes your habit to disagree without a fight. A few other suggestions are as follows:

- Stick with the subject at hand; do not go over old territory.
- Avoid using the words "never" (as in "You never....") or "always" ("Do you always have to....").
- Be unwilling to be baited into an argument by hostile language such as, "I hate you, I hate you." (You are the adult; your teen is still a child.)
- Remember that corrective conversations do not have to be fights, but correction must take place.
- It is okay for your child to have the last word. Sometimes that will prevent a power struggle.
- Do not "pick your battles." This is usually a phrase used by parents who are unwilling to correct their child on any issue: dress, music, hairstyles, curfews. If you think it is important, discuss it. Your child decides whether to make it a battle, not you. Parents should not be pulled into battle by an angry teenag-

er. Battles always cause us to say or do things we likely will regret. When things heat us to "battle" stage, it is time to separate and have a cooling off period. Parents need to demonstrate to their growing children how to do this.

Strive for corrective conversations that are kind and loving yet firm and direct. Be sure to listen honestly to your child's input while avoiding too much heat or insulting language. Be sure love is actively present throughout the correction, and you will be well on your way to honest discourse.

Will you always succeed at calm, loving disagreements? Probably not, but you will be taking the right steps to demonstrating to your child that the effort to disagree well is worth it. It opens doors for easier conversation. It keeps the family values in discussion, and it provides clarity on the expectations and consequences that the parents will enforce.

Things to Think About

- How much time do you spend talking to your children?
- Where and when do you have most of your conversations? At the dinner table? At bedtime? In the car? After school?
- Have you talked about drugs, sex and alcohol with your child? If not, could you bring these subjects up?
- If you have trouble finding talking time, what activity could you change in your family life to give you more time? Do you watch TV? Do your children participate in many structured activities? Do you or your children have much social time with other children or families? Is there one evening meeting per week you could eliminate? How much time do you or your child spend on the phone?
- How are disagreements handled in your home? Are there frequent shouting matches between siblings or

between parents and children? What steps can you take to help your children (and maybe yourself) resolve conflicts more peacefully.

Things to Do

- Pray about your conversations with your child. Ask God to give you the words that are in your heart and to make your child's heart soft and ready to hear you.
- Say goodnight to your child in her room every night.
- Eat dinner together as often as possible.
- Be reluctant to get involved or to have your child get involved in activities that will interfere with dinner or family time.
- Turn off the music in the car. Talk instead.
- Tell your child at least once every day that you love them.
- Talk about drugs, drinking and sex. You don't need to be an expert on the details, but be clear about what you believe and what the consequences for these actions would be in your household.
- Be honest, but remember that all details don't need to be told.
- Talk about God, faith, belief and their impact on your life.
- Ask open-ended questions about specifics. "How was your day today?" will yield a vague "fine." But "What did you do in English?" "Whom did you eat lunch with?" and "Did you get a chance to talk to Bob?" likely will yield more substantive answers.
- Create opportunities for shared conversation by sharing activities together. Activity can be a particularly good conversation-starter with sons: ride your bikes, shoot some baskets, run a race, play a video game together, go fishing, take a walk, go to a game. All will help open the doors to conversation.

- Remember, starting a conversation is the hardest part.
- You have two ears and one mouth; listen twice as much as you talk.

Scripture to Remember

- Deuteronomy 11:19-20 (NIV) - Teach them to your children, talking about them when you sit at home and when you walk along the road, when you lie down and when you get up. Write them on the doorframes of your houses and on your gates.
- Proverbs 22:6 - Train up a child in the way he should go, and when he is old he will not depart from it.
- Ephesians 6:4 - And you, fathers, do not provoke your children to wrath, but bring them up in the training and admonition of the Lord.

Do you believe there is an advantage to having a long view of life versus an "I want it now" mentality? Do you believe that steadfastness, loyalty or faithfulness are character qualities that your children must develop? You can influence the development of these qualities in your child. Your influence through conscious parental decision-making can promote these character traits; lazy parenting does not.

7

LEARNING to Wait

There are two middle school activities that take place in many towns and schools that reinforce the "not waiting" mentality. Unfortunately these activities are usually controlled and coordinated by adults who are well meaning and just want their children to have a great experience. One of these practices is throwing elaborate thirteen-year-old birthday parties, complete with rented room, a DJ, boys and girls together and food. This is the level of party that we might have seen even 5 years ago for children turning 16. Now it has moved down to children turning 13. What do you do for an encore at 16 if they have had the big blowout at 13? You put pressure on yourself as the parent to keep topping what you did last year, rushing your child ahead probably faster than they are ready to go. The other practice is the eighth-grade dinner dance. In some towns, the parents hire limousines to drive the eighth-grade couple back and forth to the dance. As it is, parents are spending more than $100 for a dress for their eighth-grade daughter to wear once and holding "mock-tail" parties for their 13-year-old boy and girl couples before the dance, including picture-taking.

What are these youngsters going to have to look forward to for their proms and formal dances? They have already done it all! We as parents need to slow things down so our children are not rushed headlong into adulthood before they have any of the skills or developmental abilities necessary to live like an adult.

Patience, an Acquired Attitude

Most of us are not naturally inclined to wait for what we want. Patience—or the more accurate Biblical word, longsuffering—is learned, not intuitive. If we want our children to be able to save for their future, study hard to go to a college or excel in any sport, performing art, studio art or area of study, if we want them to be able to wait for things like sexual activity, having children, getting married, then we must teach them how to delay their gratification.

This is not an easy task, since some children will develop patience earlier than others. Some personality types may be more inclined to be long-term thinkers, not in such a rush all the time. But most of us need to practice patience to learn it. As with any other lifelong lesson, we must get this practice at home.

Do you believe there is an advantage to having a long view of life versus an "I want it now" mentality? Do you believe that steadfastness, loyalty or faithfulness are character qualities that your children must develop? You can influence the development of these qualities in your child. Your influence through conscious parental decision-making can promote these character traits; lazy parenting doesn't. Don't expect to see these traits too often during the teenage years. Every now and then you will have a glimpse of patience, steadfastness and loyalty (although not always to someone you want your child to be loyal to), but we have to remember these traits take a lifetime to develop. We need to look at the end result we desire for our children when they become adults: developing the skills and commitment to a patient lifestyle over the years we have to raise them.

Live & Teach Patience

Role-model waiting for what you want. Don't indulge yourselves in everything you desire for yourself or your child. Use humor to communicate the importance of waiting. Talk about waiting for things like new cars, new furniture, going to a movie rated for an older age, playing a video game rated for someone older than you are. Start these conversations when your children are young and you are working on skills like waiting in line and sitting still. Use examples that are meaningful to your child. You wouldn't take the training wheels off her bike when she was small unless she was ready to ride a two wheeler. You don't expect a four year old to cross the street by himself. You don't allow a twelve year old to drive. How could you give approval to any activity that can harm your child if she participates before she is ready?

Role-model patience in small things wherever possible. Try the "count to ten before you say anything when you are mad" technique. Try not to tap your foot repeatedly when you are waiting in line or pound the steering wheel when you are in a rush and are suddenly stuck in traffic. What we role-model probably teaches more than anything we say.

Make your child wait for things. This sounds tough at first, but it is the best way to develop the ability to wait. If he wants $150 sneakers, have him save up half. If she wants to go to a movie rated PG-13 and she is 10, say "no" and explain that there is a time and a place for everything, and 10 is not the time for PG-13. They are not going to like this, but it is healthy for them. We want them to be able to put their own "wants" aside to meet the needs of their families in adulthood and to avoid sexual activity before they are married. We get good at waiting by waiting patiently. There truly is a time and place for everything. Some of us did not learn that until adulthood; some of us are still learning it now. We can help our child to learn this at a young age, when learning everything is a little bit easier.

Seek out other adults that will reinforce the importance of waiting for the right time. We purposely have made the choice to keep our daughter Maggie in a dance studio that makes her wait to begin a new skill or to dance in special shoes. Some studios allow the girls to begin this as young as nine or ten. Maggie's dance teacher makes the girls wait until they are thirteen, when their feet are no longer growing and their muscles are more developed in order to prevent injury. Three years seems like forever when you are performing with younger girls who seem more advanced than you, but these three years have been a wonderful experience in waiting for what she wanted. Although it has taken a lot of time in talking and reassuring, Maggie is finally, at nearly thirteen, seeing the benefit of her stronger body and more sure skills so that when we saw "little girls" (10 years old) dancing *en pointe*, she felt badly for them. No one was protecting their bodies for adulthood. I am truly grateful to her teachers for this plan.

I have to admit that I struggled with it also, having to remind myself repeatedly about the "long view" for my child. It is very easy as a parent who wants the best for her child to fall into the instant gratification trap. I found it to be helpful to have frequent talks with her teachers to remind myself that this was for the best so that I could continue to remind my daughter of the great advantage we were giving her by making her wait. Finding others who take the long view for our own child makes it much easier for us to stick with what we know is right.

Develop a strategy to make it easier to wait. It is always easier to wait for something if we distract ourselves while waiting. If you read a book while waiting for the bus, the wait goes faster. If you play cards during a long car ride, the ride goes faster. If you listen to music while you exercise, the time goes faster. How can we help our child to be distracted through the teenage years of waiting? Through healthy, active outlets for all their energy.

Long-term Activities

Encourage your child's involvement in activities at school and in the community. I'm a firm believer in little children being home with their moms. However, I also believe that once our children reach middle school, it is good for them to develop interests that they enjoy. Activities that your child loves should be encouraged, whether organized activities like classes, lessons, team activities, or individual pursuits like writing, observing nature, or art.

Trying not to let those interests interfere with family and church activities is a challenge for many of today's families. There seems to be a fine line between enough outside activities and activity overload, but somehow each family needs to find the right place. Some families recommend one activity per child; other families draw the line at activities that interfere with dinner or church; still other families want activities that occur on the weekends. In our family, our children tried a variety of different activities during their elementary school years. This may be necessary for a time to help children discover which activities fit their interests and skills. However, we found that we were spending more time running around from activity to activity than actually being able to fully enjoy any of them. So each of our children pursues one main activity year round. We as the parents have to be sure our child spends time at home for dinner, homework and just hanging around for unstructured daydreaming, reading and conversation.

We can consider some specific factors when we make choices about our children's activities starting at a young age. How do the coach and the teacher approach their teaching and training? Do they stress fundamentals? Do they consider the importance of family time and church time for practices and rehearsals? What is their philosophy? Does it agree with *your* philosophy in areas you consider to be important? How are the children treated? How much stress is involved? Does this activity enhance your child's life or just make it more complicated? Pick activities, teachers, coaches, mentors, that you as a family can live with. Be choosy.

Some activities are better at promoting delayed gratification than others. Try activities that take some time to develop, a skill that requires discipline to master, or an opportunity that allows your child to develop a relationship with someone you trust or that encourages your child to give of herself. Encourage your child to develop a relationship with a senior citizen and to listen to her. There is a wealth in the stories, character development in patience and kindness in this individual who can promote the "long view" to your child.

If your child doesn't have a specific interest or pursuit, help him find one. It is preferable that the activity be one that takes time to master. Music lessons are great teachers of delayed gratification. How about volunteering at the library or in a nursing home recreation department? Or working in the garden, growing something terrific? How about calling the local museum and becoming a guide? The ability to find an interest is only as limited as your imagination.

Rather than running down a laundry list of possible activities, get involved with your child and try some activities together—take a hike, work at the food pantry, buy groceries for the senior citizen down the street, grow something, go to a play or concert, use your local library, visit the museums. Something is bound to catch your child's attention, and who knows what will happen.

When my daughter Maggie was 7 years old, she started dancing in a local community production of the *Nutcracker*. They needed men, so my husband and my father volunteered. This quickly became a family tradition for the holidays. Now, Maggie, my husband and I, and my father all dance in the show, and my son works with the technical guys backstage. When it is all over, my stepmother throws a big cast party, and the entire family has made many new memories to be passed along. None of us ever had participated in anything like this before. We have all made many new friends. We have found we enjoy all the young people in the show immensely, and we have lots of funny stories and things to talk about at the dinner table. This is the greatest! Would I ever in a million years have imagined myself and my whole family being involved in such an extravagant undertaking? Never! One that absorbs enormous amounts of time at the holiday season? No way! But it is one of the most fun things we do together all year. It has changed our focus on the holidays—away from presents and "what I want" to the shared fun and family togetherness. We are blessed by this event every year, and we would never have been involved if we had not followed our youngest child's lead. Let your child lead you to something new. You won't be sorry!

Waiting for Dating

I recommend that teens wait to date until sixteen. This gives our daughters time to mature and formulate their thinking on boys and sexual activity. It gives us time to communicate about sexual decision-making before they fall in love. It gives them time to develop the words to say to the boys they date about how far they will go.

This gives our sons time to begin to manage impulse control, something very hard for them when testosterone is new in their bodies at the onset of puberty. It allows them time to be boys without the macho pressure of sexual activity. It gets our sons off the hook in the dating world. Many boys are in no rush to date, but they feel compelled to because it is what their friends are doing.

It allows both our sons and daughters to spend time with each other in a group, feeling somewhat more freedom to be themselves, not to try to be what the "date" wants them to be. It also gives our children a chance to spend time with a wide variety of other children so that they have a chance to decide what type of person they want to spend time with.

The later our child starts dating, the easier it will be for her to wait until marriage to become sexually active. You are more likely to become a sexually active teen if you are dating, kissing, touching each other's bodies as an eighth grader than if you don't begin these behaviors until junior year in high school.

At minimum we should allow our children to date only those in their grade or class at school. We should pay particular attention to dating activity between junior and senior boys in high school and freshman girls. Without my meaning to be sexist, we have to pay very close attention when the freshman is a daughter. High school teachers tell me there are not four years difference in maturity between freshman girls and senior boys, but forty years! Without even being conscious of it, a young man can easily manipulate an immature, wanting-to-please freshman into going further than she intends. The hardest part of this is that our daughters truly believe that they have a handle on the situation and that they won't allow anything to happen that they don't want. We as parents know the challenge she will face when her boyfriend treats her in a way that makes her feel older and special.

A common question children ask me is, "What happens if you decide to wait and your partner doesn't?" The girls particularly seem concerned that they will wait and wait until they are twenty-five, and then fall in love with someone who didn't wait at all. This is how I manage this concern: If you decide to wait, you are going to give the people that you date some information about yourself. One piece of that information is that you are going to wait to have sex. What I suggest saying is, "There is something I'd like you to know about me. I am waiting until I am married to have sex. I hope you will respect that." I tell them to say this on the phone, at McDonald's, while taking a walk, at any time that they are not alone and tempted. Actually this conversation should take place before they are alone. It is much harder to begin this conversation about how far you will go when you are swept up in the excitement of hugging and kissing.

By telling this to the people that you date, you immediately narrow the pool of people you will date long-term. You will be dating people that are interested in you as a person and people who have the ability to wait for what they want. This counts. Remember, you will marry someone that you date. If you want to marry someone who is steadfast, patient and faithful, you need to date people who are steadfast, patient and faithful. By letting your potential partners know you are waiting to have sex, you screen out all the immature, impatient, "have to have it now" kind of people. If the person your child is dating understands the value of saving sex until marriage, then he likely will have the character and honesty that you have reinforced in your child.

Now, the truth is that your child may fall in love and decide to marry someone who hasn't decided to wait. Maybe he made choices when he was young, and he's changed his mind. Maybe he never thought about waiting until he met your child, fell in love and learned the value of waiting for what you want. This can happen. People make mistakes; people change. What then? The advantage is that only one of them has a sexual history, so that decreases by half the risk they would experience if both of them were previously sexually active. The disadvantage is the risk of sexually transmitted disease is present because of your child's partner's sexual history. Testing is important at this stage, so that any treatable diseases can be treated and the inexperienced partner has full awareness of the risks associated with sexual intimacy. The decision is completely your child's to make. It is best to have as much information as possible when making such an important decision. If your child chooses to marry someone with a sexually transmitted disease, she can learn how to manage her sex life to decrease the risk of transmission and decrease the risk of complications.

Waiting becomes a state of mind. It influences our approach to many areas of our lives: family, work, recreation. (Even spontaneous fun is best if it's planned–your backyard picnic is more delightful if there is delicious food in the house to choose from, and your long hike in the woods is most comfortable if you have the right shoes to wear.) Also our spiritual lives are affected by a patient, steadfast approach to our life as a whole. Even though we live in a culture that promotes instant gratification for every area of our lives, as we mature, we see the benefit of "slow and steady." The childhood story of the tortoise and the hare has more than just a kernel of truth to it. We may not have the glamour in waiting. We may not experience the rush of adrenaline that is so valued by our culture today. But we will stay healthy. We will succeed over the long haul, and we will be able to have meaning and depth in our relationships with others. These take time. Let's show our children how to take that time and use it to grow into joyful, stable, fulfilled adults.

Things to Think About

- How good are you at waiting for what you want?
- Do you push the elevator button 10 times before it comes?
- How often do you change channels with the remote during commercials?
- Do you make prudent financial decisions?
- What do you think is worth waiting for?
- Does your child receive everything she wants?
- Do you ever make your child wait for something? Do you talk about waiting? Do you ever delay an answer or a consequence?
- Do you feel bad when you say "no"? Does this ever cause you to change your mind?

Things to Do

- Pray about God's desires for your children with regards to waiting. Ask Him for the words you need to talk about this subject with them.
- Talk about waiting. What makes it hard? What can make it easier?
- Establish guidelines for dating, seeing movies or playing video games that are rated older than your child. Stick to them.
- Help your child to choose activities that develop long-

term thinking, self-discipline and self-control. Examples include playing an instrument, planting a garden, studying nature, writing, sports, becoming fluent in another language, pursuing science, performing in the arts.
- Begin an activity as a family: hiking in the woods, going to museums, attending concerts and plays, keeping baseball scores.
- Give your child something to wait for: a new computer game, expensive sneakers, a trip to the mall with you.
- Examine your habits with regards to waiting. Do you wait well? Are you always in a hurry? Do you want today what you wanted yesterday? What can you change to be a better role model for your child?
- Establish dating guidelines even if your children are only in fifth grade.

Scripture to Remember

- Psalm 27:14 - Wait on the Lord, be of good courage and He shall strengthen your heart.
- Psalm 37:7 - Rest in the Lord and wait patiently for Him.
- Lamentations 3:25-26 - The Lord is good to those who wait for Him, to the soul who seeks Him. It is good that one should hope and wait quietly for the salvation of the Lord.
- Ecclesiastes 7:8 - The patient in spirit is better than the proud in spirit.
- 1 Corinthians 3:10 - I have laid the foundation and another builds on it. But let each one take heed how he builds on it.
- Hebrews 10:36 - For you have need of endurance, so that after you have done the will of God, you may receive the promise.
- James 5:7-8 - Therefore be patient, brethren, until the coming of the Lord. See how the farmer waits for the

precious fruit of the earth.... You also be patient. Establish your hearts, for the coming of the Lord is at hand.

- Romans 12:12 (NIV) - Be joyful in hope, patient in affliction, faithful in prayer.

Statistically speaking, 20% of teens will be sexually active no matter what, and 20% of teens will not be sexually active no matter what. That leaves 60% of teens that can be influenced one way or the other. . . . The most important factor in delaying sexual activity in teens is parental disapproval.

8

SEX, Delay or Pay

The first teen mom I ever worked with was referred to me in the middle of a custody dispute. She was fighting for custody of her baby from her boyfriend's parents. When this fifteen year old told her parents she was pregnant, they told her she had to move out of the house and take care of the baby herself. In my experience, this is the most common parental response to pregnancy. She was living in substandard housing with another young mom and her baby. She was welfare dependent for housing, money, food and health care. She had broken up with her boyfriend, but he was involved with the baby and her on and off as he was able. He also was a young teen. They fought loudly and frequently. In order to go to school, she was leaving her baby with people that she knew who helped her out, but who were also troubled, unemployed, and substance abusing. One day her baby had a large bruise on her head; another day she had injuries to her legs. The baby was being abused by the caregivers. The paternal grandparents volunteered to take custody of the baby and launched a custody battle. They stated that the teen mom used poor judgment, allowed the abuse to happen and, therefore, was unfit to raise the baby. She eventually lost custody and moved out of the area. I don't know if she ever regained custody or if she even tried. But it was a sad reality of life for a girl too young to have a baby and the toll it takes on everyone involved.

Dose of Reality

A fact of life for teens today is that many of them will have the opportunity to have sex before they are married. Most of them will have the chance before they graduate from high school. Forty-two percent of our children will take advantage of that chance to become sexually active before the end of freshman year.[1] As with alcohol and drug use, we look at the freshman year as the first big year of risk.

Generally speaking, 20% of teens will be sexually active no matter what, and 20% of teens will not be sexually active no matter what. That leaves 60% of teens that can be influenced one way or the other. The good news here is that the most important factor in delaying sexual activity in teens is parental disapproval. For the many reasons, I will discuss in this chapter, I am hopeful we can begin consciously to influence our children to wait until marriage for sexual activity.

The decision to have sex is actually a more important life decision than the decision to go to college. It is a more life-*changing* decision because it is a decision that is more difficult to erase and start fresh again. The regrets are likely to be longer lasting. When I think of all the hours of time and effort we have spent poring over college books, taking tours, talking endlessly at the dinner table about college and the future, I wonder how many of us put that kind of effort into helping our children make other life-changing decisions as well.

There are four things we need to consider in order to make a good decision:

1. *Make your important decisions in advance.*

You don't decide whom you are going to marry the morning of the wedding. You don't decide where to go to college the Labor Day after you graduate from high school. You think about these things for years before you decide. We want our children to think that far in advance about sex also. You can transfer from one college to the next. You can go further away or closer to home, or you can switch to a bigger or smaller school and experience no harm. With sex, it is possible, even likely, that you will experience a severe consequence the first time you have sex. In a 1999 survey by *Seventeen* magazine, 80% of sexually active teenage girls regret their sexual activity. This is a consequence that leads to depression, loss of self-respect and sexual promiscuity. With so much at stake, it is crucial to guide children in making the decision well in advance.

2. *Know your feelings.*

Feelings are VERY important. They drive much of our human response. Feelings are very intense during adolescence and need to be recognized. As parents, we must be very careful not to put down our children's feelings but to help them manage them effectively. Before our children become sexually active, it is necessary for them to know how they feel.

When your child is looking for college, you are going to visit schools. At some schools, your child barely will get out of the car, yet he will not "feel" right about a school. So you'll drive away. At other schools, your child is going to get out of the car and say, "I love it here. This is where I want to go." That's the feeling! But we also must know, Can you get in? Are your SAT scores good enough? Can we afford it? Do they offer your major?

Likewise, with decisions about sex, "feelings" may begin the process, but much more must be considered before getting involved in a relationship at this level: Do they love this person and think they will be together for the rest of their lives? Do they like this person and feel that it is time to become sexually active? Do they feel pressure from their friends and just want to get it over with? (This one is very common.) Are they both just drinking too much and, now, simply are too convenient for each other?

*3.   Understand that your feelings don't offer enough informa-
    tion.*

All our feelings tell us is how we feel. They don't tell us
if this is a good or bad decision. They don't tell us anything
at all about the other person. (Although our daughters are
likely to think that if they are in love, their boyfriends are
also. We all know this isn't necessarily true. Think of the old
"Men are from Mars, Women are from Venus" story.) One of
the skills we want our children to learn is how not to act sole-
ly on their feelings. As with college-hunting, we must gather
our facts, particularly because the feelings are so strong. We
have to gather the facts about sexual activity to help to coun-
terbalance the strength of those feelings.

*4.   Never, ever, ever, under any circumstances change how you
    feel and then make an important decision like having sex.*

The purpose of drugs and alcohol is to change how you
feel. If they didn't change our feelings, no one would drink or
use drugs. If we alter our feelings with substances and t h e n
make an important decision about sex, I can promise you
that this is a decision that will cause regret. This is a huge
challenge for teens today, not just throughout high school
but during college and young adulthood as well.

What is the difference between a good decision and a bad
one? A good decision takes us closer to our future instead of
further away from it. It will enhance the peace in your home
instead of taking away from it. It will prevent you from keeping serious secrets away from the people who care for you and
take care of you. A good decision is easier to make if we take
a look at some of the factors involved.

To Be Sexually Active or Not?

Consequences of Waiting

First, look at the problems children think they will face when they choose not to be sexually active. When I speak to the teenagers, we work on the "logic tree." In the logic tree, we write all the problems you may experience if you don't have sex on the right side of the board and all the problems you may face if you have sex on the left. The students raise their hands and give me the answers, which I write on the board. This gives the teens a chance to visually recognize the factors involved in making the decision about sexual activity. There is remarkable similarity in the answers from school to school and town to town. The eighth and ninth graders I work with share the same kinds of anxieties and pressures no matter where they live or what their parents do for a living. No matter what the economic status, their neighborhood, the school they attend, or the church or school program, teens are all facing pressures from the same dilemmas.

Internal pressure

*The most common concern of students who are not sexually active is **pressure**.*

The pressure boys feel to be sexually active is crushing. They think about sex constantly, and they talk about their sex lives with their friends. They don't all tell the truth in the talking, but on some level they believe each other. That is the source of great pressure. Younger boys think the pressure which they will experience will all be external, but we have to help prepare them for the internal pressure as well—the pressure that makes them ask themselves, "Why isn't this happening to me?" The life of a sexually active friend seems very exciting, especially when heard through his own storytelling.

This pressure comes from the simple fact that children discuss their sex lives. If your child views sex as something private and personal, then she can't be sexually active during the teen years because sex is neither private nor personal in high school. Sex is a free conversation in high school, and the reality is that what "everyone knows" probably is not accurate. But everyone believes them anyhow. As a matter of fact, when I am with the students, it is very common for them all to look towards the children in the group that are sexually active, or at least perceived as such. I go to high schools in which girls' names are passed around on a list that not only tells how "far" the girls will go but also whether they are any good at it or not. This happens in high schools in which the parents would have absolutely no idea this type of activity occurs within their child's peer group. It opens our most personal and private self up for the whole world (as high school is for its students) to see. We must raise our sons to be much more manly and respectful than this. We must raise our daughters to never allow themselves to be put in the position in which they will be discussed in this degrading way.

I suggest to youth, boys and girls alike, that they develop a personal policy of not discussing their sex lives. This is honorable. I tell them not to say, "I won't discuss my sex life because I don't have one" or "I won't discuss my sex life because it is so good you'll die of jealousy," but instead simply "I don't talk about my sex life" or some humorous take on that statement. Once our child decides not to discuss his sex life, he can relieve some pressure from himself because no one else will know what he is or is not doing. It becomes a personal decision—just how it should be.

There is also the internal pressure of **wanting**.

This pressure is experienced by boys and girls alike. The feelings of the teenage years are very strong. If our children aren't prepared to wait for what they want, this wanting pressure overwhelms them, and they don't even bother to think through the decision. They just go with what they want. Who could blame them? They have not learned yet how to wait if their families haven't provided the opportunity for them to practice waiting. See chapter 7 for some ideas about how to help our children learn how to wait.

*The internal pressure and the pressure of wanting are compounded by the influence of the **popular culture**.*

This influence is great, and it is more subtle than we imagine. So an entire chapter is devoted to this. See chapter 9.

External pressures

*There are also the external pressures of **what others will think**.*

The boys worry about their friends. The children tell me they are afraid people will think they are gay, they are afraid, or they are "wusses." They are right. Children do talk about each other; boys tease each other relentlessly about their manhood. It happens. (The concept of being afraid of being called "gay," or using that term in a bullying way, is indeed an issue, but it is beyond the scope of this book.) We have to help our sons live with this, not allow this teasing to force them into a decision that may harm them. By their junior year of high school, most children are able to live comfortably with their choice to wait. So we just have to help our sons get to that point of maturity.

The girls worry about the boys. They worry about their popularity and whether anyone will ask them out. We need to help our daughters realize that there are more important reasons to be asked out than sex. What about having boys ask you out because you are nice or funny or say smart things in class? How about because you seem shy and quiet or that you always know how to make someone laugh or that you share an interest like music or sports or theatre? Shouldn't those be the reasons you'd like boys to like you? If you become known for having sex, the boys will never know all those other great things about you. They will know only how good you are at sex. The double standard is still alive and well in high schools in every town. The boys will have sex with some girls and date others. It never works for girls to get involved in a relationship by having sex first. Please be sure your daughter knows this as well as she knows her name. This is a very big mistake that many girls make. Her heart is broken when the boy doesn't become her boyfriend, and she cannot go back to undo the damage to her self-respect.

One day, in a large, coed group of juniors in high school, I said to the girls, "Raise your hand if you would prefer to date a boy who doesn't put pressure on you to have sex." Every single girl in the audience raised her hand! I barely had the sentence out, and they were raising their hands. Our sons need to know that girls prefer to be with boys who don't put pressure on them to have sex. They believe that girls will think less of them if they don't pursue sex in the relationship. I began routinely to ask this question when I was with a large group, and I found girls everywhere who tell me this is not so. They like to have boyfriends; they love to be with the boys, but they don't want the pressure. They just want to have the fun, have the relationship, and just enjoy them as a person. They want their boyfriends to do the same for them. So boys who say to girls, "I want you to know something. I'm not going to put pressure on you to have sex in this relationship," are the boys who have the girls crazy about them.

I asked the boys the same question, and most of the boys' hands went up. I was surprised and admitted my sexism to them. I said, "Wow, I'm surprised. I didn't think you boys felt the same way." One young man, a mature junior in high school raised his hand and said,

I want to be really clear about this. There are two kinds of girls: girls we date and girls we have sex with. They are not the same girls. If I'm going to have a girl as my girlfriend, I can't trust her if she just wants to be having sex all the time. What's different about me than the other guys? But if I want to have a girl that's my girlfriend, I want to have a girl who enjoys me for exactly who I am.

Becoming sexually active during a long-term relationship is more likely to harm the relationship than help it. Once a girl is sexually active with her boyfriend, she starts to have different expectations of him. She feels that she has given him something precious about herself. She has. Most girls don't understand how important sex will be to them until they become sexually active. Physiological changes that take place in a woman during sexual intimacy cause her to release the hormone oxytocin, which is the hormone that promotes bonding. A teenage girl has no evidence that her boyfriend has bonded to her unless he attends to her in a special way. Once she makes this choice, she wants him to call her, sit with her at lunch, and spend more time with her exclusively. Frankly, considering the risk she puts herself in every time she has sex, it seems to me—from a woman's perspective—that the least she should expect of him is his time.

In his mind he is just a teenage boy. He wants to be with his friends; he doesn't want to be committed to anything. He feels young and free and doesn't want the pressure of paying that much attention to one girl. He didn't realize having sex was going to complicate things; he probably doesn't like the demands very much. They worry about pregnancy, and they worry about being caught. The relationship is suddenly more difficult and maybe not worth the effort. They may argue more and eventually break up.

Surveys of relationships show that teens are much more likely to break up if they are sexually active than if they decide to wait. Several years ago, a social psychology class in a very large public high school conducted a survey for me. Their job was to find students who had broken up because one of a couple did not want to have sex. They developed a survey that camouflaged their intent and asked most of the more than 2,000 students in their school for the reasons they had broken up with past girlfriends and boyfriends. They found many couples who had broken up because of jealousy, pregnancy, cheating on each other, dislike of the demands of the relationship, distrust, poor treatment of one partner by the other, loss of interest in each other, or going different ways. But they didn't find one student who had broken up because one partner wanted to have sex and the other didn't. I see the students in this school every year, and I tell them about this survey. Two years ago I had the first student ever raise her hand to tell me her boyfriend broke up with her because she would not have sex with him. I empathized with her for the heartache that must have caused. She told us in front of her entire class that she was heartbroken at first. Then her ex-boyfriend broke up with his next girlfriend because she was pregnant. So she feels that she made the best decision possible. Yes, she lost the boy, but he was a boy worth losing. At least she had her dignity, her virginity and her self-respect intact because she made the right decision.

The right decision is often difficult to make at first, but it also will prove itself as a good choice over the long run. If our children have a relationship they want to preserve and nurture, becoming sexually active prevents them from sustaining the relationship because they no longer would have the respect. We can tell our children this honestly and with great respect for the importance of their feelings for each other.

Asking our children to wait to be sexually active is a true sign of our trust in our child, our respect for our child, and our belief that our child is deserving of happy, healthy relationships with the opposite sex. What we understand, because we have the "long view" which our teen has not yet developed, is that being sexually active will harm relationships and bring less happiness, not just now but in the years ahead as well. Talk about this with your children. Help them see the value in relationships that last a long time.

CONSEQUENCES OF SEXUAL ACTIVITY

Now, we fill the left side of the board. While the challenges of waiting are compelling and the teens appreciate an understanding of the difficulties, both internal and external, it is the difficulties that occur as a result of sexual activity that are life changing, primarily in a negative way by adding complications to an already complicated stage of life.

The thing your children worry about the most is *you*. They worry about getting caught. They worry about something happening and their parents' finding out. They want their parents to have a good opinion of them. They understand that coming to you with a problem as a result of sexual activity may change your good opinion. This supports research by the Alan Guttmacher Institute, the research arm of Planned Parenthood, that tells us the number one factor in the prevention of teen pregnancy is perceived parental disapproval. This is a notable, if not unexpected, result from this organization.

Sexually Transmitted Diseases

Sexually active teens need to worry about sexually transmitted diseases (STD's). STD's are the most common diseases in America next to the common cold and flu. Daily 33,000 new cases are reported. Sixty three percent of all STD's occur in teenagers. Although there are more than 50 different sexually transmitted diseases (STD's) we are only going to discuss seven of them. These seven are the most common STD's among teenagers, and all but one of them are totally preventable with the practice of chastity. Our daughters are particularly at risk, not just for the diseases themselves but because the consequences can be much worse for a teenage girl. Her reproductive tract produces more mucus, therefore, better food for the bacteria or virus, encouraging it to spread more rapidly throughout her vagina, cervix and uterus.

Human papilloma virus

HPV, or *human papilloma virus*, is one of the most common STD's. One out of every three sexually active teenagers

113

acquires HPV during the course of their sexual activity. According to the Centers for Disease Control, an estimated 75% of the reproductive aged population has been infected with HPV.[2] Forty million people are thought to be carriers of this disease. This is a virus, not a curable bacteria. So once your child acquires this disease, she is likely to have it for the rest of her life.

I was reminded of how common and devastating this disease is when we were making our videotape. As the production crew was setting up for the taping at our medium-sized community hospital, they needed to vacate the auditorium for an OB/GYN meeting to take place. As the doctors came in, they wondered what all the equipment was for. As they got into conversation with the crew about the subject of our video, one of the doctors commented on how he had to have a conversation with me: Did you know about the devastating effects of the disease HPV? He wanted to be sure that our children were warned about the terrible consequences of this disease. He believes that he sees far too much cervical cancer, a disease which can be thwarted by decreasing the amount of unmarried sex that our children are participating in. This is one of those "long view" situations. Like many of the other diseases we will discuss, the consequences of HPV occur later in life, not at the time of acquiring the disease.

The symptom of this virus is genital warts, but most of the teens who acquire this virus will not get the warts. So they have no way of knowing that they have caught it. Between 1.3 and 13% of those with HPV have genital warts at any given time.[3] Many women whose warts are internal, vaginal warts do not know they have this virus until they have an abnormal pap smear. This information is devastating to hear for adult women. For teens who may be trying to keep their sexual activity a secret, it is even worse. HPV is responsible for nearly 90% of all pre-cancerous lesions of the cervix.[4] Cervical cancer is the second most common cancer for women worldwide, taking more lives than HIV as recently as

1995[5] and is directly related to sexual activity. Consider also that condoms do not stop the spread of this disease, and we begin to see the tangible dangers of sexual activity for our teens. This is a skin-to-skin transmitted disease that leaves its host feeling dirty, unworthy, or contaminated.

After working with the peer leaders in a large urban high school, I was approached by a very cute girl. She was a peer leader at the top of her class of more than 750, had been accepted at MIT, and was very excited about her future. She wanted to talk to me because she was afraid that she had genital warts even though she had never had sex. It seems that she and her boyfriend were "doing everything but sex," and this included lying naked with each other. She was trying sincerely to do the right thing in avoiding sex but was unsure of where to draw the line between desire and safety. She loved her boyfriend and believed that he had never been sexually active before. *This belief about him turned out not to be true.* I sent her to be tested; a pap test will usually pick this up since HPV is transmitted by skin-to-skin contact, not through body fluids. She tested positive; she was devastated. Her view of herself as a good girl was changed; she felt unclean, unlovable and betrayed. Here was a lovely young woman about to enter into a wondrous stage of her life, and she was left feeling dirty and depressed because of a disease she never should have acquired.

Chlamydia

Another very common, symptomless disease is *chlamydia.* Between 20% and 40% of sexually active females will acquire this infection.[6] Boys acquire it also but without the devastating effects. While this is treatable fairly easily with antibiotics, you have to know you have it to have it treated. Most teens do not view themselves as high risk for sexually transmitted diseases. They don't seek health care, and, therefore, they remain undiagnosed. Chlamydia spreads easily throughout the reproductive tract, causing scarring, which leads to infertility. Many women don't realize they have chlamydia until they seek treatment for infertility or Pelvic Inflammatory Disease (PID). About 75% of women who have chlamydia that has spread will require surgery to conceive. The first infection causes a 25% chance of infertility; the second infection leads to a 50% chance.[7] What a terrible consequence for a young woman who will likely break up with the boy who gave her the chlamydia within 6 months of beginning their sexual activity. Because chlamydia is a skin-to-skin transmitted disease, condoms also will not stop the spread of this disease.

When I managed the adolescent pregnancy project, I occasionally would receive letters from couples hoping to adopt a baby from one of our teen moms (who very rarely release their babies for adoption). These heartbreaking letters would include some of the most personal information imaginable: how much money the couple made, how they spend their private time, religious affiliation, political interests, where they live, what their extended families are like, and what they hope and plan for the future. It was not uncommon for me to receive pictures of the couple, their house, or their pets. These letters were a marketing tool for infertile couples whose strongest desire was to start a family. The most likely cause of their infertility is chlamydia. When we consider the terrible toll chlamydia takes on a woman's reproductive tract, we must understand that our child could end up writing one of these letters if chlamydia becomes a part of her life. The only way for our teens to avoid chlamydia is by avoiding premature, unmarried sexual activity.

Genital herpes

Genital herpes is the third most common STD in teens. The Center for Disease Control estimates that one out of every five Americans over the age of 12 has genital herpes.[8]

More than one million cases are reported every year.[9] It is a virus that is acquired most often during adolescence and young adulthood.[10] There is no cure, and our children will be responding to the problems of herpes for the rest of their lives. Our children see commercials on TV for herpes medicine and think it is a cure. There is no cure. The medicine will decrease the length of time a sufferer will experience the sores, and it will lengthen the time between breakouts. But it will not cure herpes.

Genital herpes causes cold sore-like breakouts on the genitals. These are quite painful, crusty, red, oozing. Herpes can be spread before the sores are visible, so our teens need to understand they cannot look at their partner to determine whether or not they have this or any other sexually transmitted disease.

Women with genital herpes may need to have a Caesarean section to deliver their babies to prevent the spread of the virus to the baby during birth. If the virus spreads it can be fatal to the baby.[11] When I worked in obstetrics, the most unhappy women I spoke with had just had a Caesarean section because their husbands gave them herpes. They were in isolation (in a private room where caregivers have to wear gloves). Many of these women were feeling humiliation at their situation, in which they found themselves due to their husbands' earlier choices in life. Today, our daughters are at risk for making this choice, which leads to regret. Imagine the sadness of having your birth experience altered because of a disease you picked up from someone you don't even know any more. We need to let our girls understand the very common risk they take with the choice to be sexually active. Our sons need to understand the emotional toll on their marriage should they spread this disease to their wife, a disease they caught from a past relationship, that will bring challenge to the relationship that matters the most: their marriage.

HIV

Any sexually active person has to worry about the virus known as *HIV*. According to a report in the *Journal of the American Medical Association* in March 1997, this disease is transmitted most commonly today through heterosexual (men and women together) contact. In my home state of Connecticut teenage females are the fastest growing group of HIV-positive people. There continues to be the thinking within teenage groups that HIV is a homosexual disease. Even with all the health education our children are receiving, somehow this fact eludes them. It may be naïve thinking of adolescence at work. ALL those who are sexually active outside of a permanent relationship are at risk for being infected with HIV, which is a fatal disease.

The HIV virus lives and multiplies in the immune system, gradually taking over until the body no longer has the ability to fight infection. There are medications which can slow this process down and boost the immune system, but as yet there are no medications to cure HIV. Our children are at risk for contracting this deadly disease if they choose to be sexually active. There are one million Americans infected with this disease. Twenty percent, or 200,000, are young adults. Twenty percent of everyone infected with this disease are infected during their teenage years.

HIV can be spread through oral sex. Our children have the notion that oral sex is "safe" sex. They are wrong. The only problem avoided with oral sex is pregnancy. There remains the risk for the sexually transmitted diseases, including HIV. These organisms are not picky about how they get into the body; they just want to get in. Wherever there is an opening, the organisms can make their way into the body. If the opening is in the mouth because the teeth have been brushed or flossed, or maybe there is a pizza burn or a sharp cracker or chip, and she has someone else's reproductive body fluids in her mouth and those fluids have a sexually transmitted disease in them, she can catch the disease.

Our children are engaging in oral sex at younger and younger ages. You may have read articles about children as young as sixth grade participating in oral sex "parties." In my own experience, children start talking to me about these parties in eighth grade. These parties involve several children—boys and girls. The girls give the boys oral sex without leaving the room; they are all together when this occurs. All kinds of children at many different kinds of schools and communities participate in this activity. (This is another reason why parties need to be closely supervised.) Somehow, they don't view oral sex as intimate; they argue very strongly with me that oral sex isn't even "sex." Of course it is! When you have someone's genitals in your mouth you are having sex. If it weren't sex, it would be called oral "something else," but it's not. It is called oral "sex" for a reason.

Gonorrhea and syphilis

Gonorrhea and *syphilis* have been around the longest and are still going strong. More than one half million new cases of gonorrhea are diagnosed every year and more than 75,000 new cases of syphilis.[12]

Syphilis is the disease checked for in the premarital blood test and in all newly pregnant women, as women often are symptom-less for the first stage. Syphilis causes damage to the brain and nervous system, and it causes serious birth defects or even newborn death. Men may experience a swollen, non-painful ulcer on their penis or testicles, but this usually will go away on its own. However, the syphilis has not gone away, just the symptom. Syphilis is curable with antibiotics, but you have to know you have it to go in for treatment. The routine testing helps to catch some cases that would go otherwise unknown. Syphilis is the only STD that has routine testing.

Gonorrhea is often symptom-less for women. They may have some pelvic pain and pain when they urinate, but they are as likely not to. Men have burning during urination and a greenish, thick, pus-like discharge from the penis. Like chlamydia, gonorrhea causes infertility by scarring the reproductive tracts of men and women. Like chlamydia and syphilis, this disease is also curable with antibiotics. As it may be more likely to have symptoms, it may be more likely to be treated, especially for men.

Hepatitis B

Hepatitis B causes a non-curable liver disease. This is the only STD on the list that has a vaccine. Your children should be vaccinated for this during their routine vaccinations. It is a three-shot series definitely worth having. Hepatitis B is the most common STD in the world. Even if you feel sure your child is not going to be sexually active—a dangerous assumption—you should be sure that he or she has the hepatitis B vaccine. It is possible to pick this up via contaminated food or water, though not as commonly as by sexual contact.

This short list of sexually transmitted diseases is full of unfortunate consequences for teens who choose to be sexually active. My experience with teens has taught me how few of our children believe they would experience an STD even when they are sexually active. The moment-to-moment thinking of adolescence allows them to believe they will not get hurt even when participating in high-risk behaviors.

Since most teens who have an STD don't have any symptoms, most don't know they have it. The children who know they have the disease are unlikely to talk about it even with their closest friends. If our teen doesn't know anyone who has it, he doesn't believe anyone else has an STD. There is no feedback in our teens' cultural experience that convinces them that sexual activity is risky. Just watch one evening of your teen's favorite TV shows, and you'll see lots of implied sexual activity without any consequences. Our children somehow unconsciously believe that what they see on TV is true. On one level they know it is just entertainment, but on another level they are trusting that what they see is true. This makes it harder for our children to understand the true risk of sexual activity.

Pregnancy

Our children also have to worry about pregnancy if they choose to be sexually active. Our sons need to be as concerned about this potential problem as our daughters, though our daughters bear the physical burden of the pregnancy.

When I am with students in eighth grade and up, I give them homework about pregnancy. Their job is to have a conversation at the dinner table about what would happen in their house if they as young ladies, or their girlfriends as young men, were to become pregnant. Their reports on this event vary widely and sometimes are very funny. Sometimes the answers break my heart. Some girls come in and report that their mother told them they would have an abortion. Some girls come in and say they would get kicked out of their house. Some boys come in and say that their parents viewed this as their girlfriends' problem, not theirs. Some dads tell their sons they would pay for the girl to have an abortion. Some children "jokingly" say their parents would kill them. One boy said, "I would never tell my mother in the kitchen. That's where we keep the knives." Many say their parents would expect them to live up to their responsibility.

On page 122 is a letter written by a mom to her eighth-grade daughter. Her daughter thought the letter was so special that she gave me a copy and asked me to read it out loud to her classmates. I almost can promise you that this girl will not have a pregnancy as a teenager. Her mom loves her in a way that allows the daughter to be responsible for her actions but continue to feel loved. I would guess this mother prayed before writing this poignant and potentially life-saving letter.

Pregnancy is a consequence of intercourse that will change the course of your child's life forever, no matter what the result of the pregnancy is. Our daughters will have to live

Dear _____,

If you came home and told me you were pregnant, I would:

1. *Feel so bad that I let you down not making you understand the dangers of having sex as a teenager.*
2. *Try to be as supportive as possible, knowing that your life as you know it was pretty much over.*
3. *Get up with you every morning and rub your back while you threw up.*
4. *Make you feel better when you didn't want to go out in public as you were getting noticeably more pregnant.*
5. *Sit home with you on weekend nights while your friends were out at parties or the movies.*
6. *Experience heartbreak for you as you started to love this baby inside of you, knowing that you could never give her the life she deserved.*
7. *Go to your doctor's appointments with you so you wouldn't be alone while everyone was staring and whispering.*
8. *Hold your hand while you were drenched in sweat, in labor, having the worst pain of your life, praying like you've never prayed before that you could take it all back.*
9. *Encourage you to give this baby up for adoption to give her a chance for a normal life with 2 parents who could afford and desperately wanted a child.*
10. *Feel so bad for you as you spent endless nights awake, wondering where your baby was, if she was happy, and if she would ever know that she had another mom.*
11. *Hope that eventually you could forgive yourself and begin to get on with your life.*
12. *Most of all, hope that you were smart enough to figure this all out ahead of time so that none of this would ever happen.*

Letter from a mom to her eighth-grade daughter

with any decision they make. Not one solution is an easy one or will leave our girls unharmed physically, emotionally or spiritually. They have three choices.

Option 1: Carry the pregnancy to term and raise the baby.

One solution for a teen mom is to raise her baby at home with her family. While not ideal, teen moms have more success when they can stay at home than when they try to raise the baby alone. This requires a lot of family support, including the physical support of childcare until she is through with college. In order eventually to support herself and her baby, the teen mom must finish high school and go to college or other post-high school training to obtain a job that will allow her to become independent. This is a long difficult road for the entire family that takes place for fewer than 25% of teenage mothers. A teen pregnancy creates tension in even the most relaxed and informal households. There will be a new mouth to feed, a new person to house, and a new schedule to keep. The physical disruption of a newborn in the house with all the equipment and supplies that a baby needs and the schedule challenges of a baby that is up at night, perhaps waking up everyone (including the little siblings of the teen mom and her parents), can leave everyone in the family on edge.

The emotional toll is also very high: the feelings the parents have about what got their daughter into this situation in the first place, the conflict or undercurrent of unhappiness about the changes in everyone's lives, the embarrassment felt by all members of the family. The young mom feels enormous pressure about all of this, but she is primarily concerned about the changes that will occur in her life. Conflict is inevitable. It is very common for the baby's father to be out of the picture by the time the baby is born, and this causes distress for the teen mom. Often there is much unhappiness and disagreement as the teen parents are breaking up and adjusting to their changes.

With all this going on, your daughter has to get back to school and the resulting social changes that come with her new responsibilities. She may feel differently about her friends; her friends may feel differently about her. Certainly, she is not invited to bring her baby to parties and dances or to just hang around with her friends. This can be very lonely. If she had been involved in sports or other extracurricular activities, she now has to take care of her first responsibility, her baby. So she no longer has time for meetings and practices that might keep her after school. She has to try to keep up with her schoolwork despite all the changes, the lack of sleep, the worries, the needs of the baby, the financial concerns, the differences with her boyfriend, her grief over her old way of life. Her days of carefree, or at least care-*less*, childhood have come to an end.

There are inevitable conflicts when a teen is living at home and has a baby. Who truly parents the baby? The grandparents or the teen parent? It takes enormous self-control on the part of the grandparents (the parent of the teen mom or dad) to allow their child to raise the baby. Where do we as the grandparents draw the line between supporting our child and becoming the parents to our grandchild? Power struggles are likely when you complicate the challenge every teen has with emancipation with the dependency that comes along with being a teen parent. All parties walk a very thin tightrope when parents are trying to be supportive of their teen who is a parent. We cannot allow our children, who are now parents, to continue as children, though they are.

What about our sons who father a child? They must fulfill their fatherly responsibilities, which are not limited to financial support. A father needs to be present for his child. His baby needs to know who his father is as he grows up. He needs to know his dad will be there for him, take care of him, play with him, read to him, be kind to his mother.

Your son has to find a way to rise to his new level of responsibility while still moving forward with his schoolwork.

He must find a way to support the family he has already started, while continuing to prepare for college, which now has to be somewhere near where his baby is going to be. That could change his college choices, and he has no say in where his baby might be living. It is likely he will at some point in his life be supporting two families and two households, so he needs to be sure he can get and keep a job that will provide him with the financial resources to do this. He is going to have to treat the mother of his baby well, show her kindness and support, even if they no longer are boyfriend and girlfriend, because they are going to be co-parenting their child for THE REST OF THEIR LIVES. Even when they both have new spouses and children, they will be permanently connected through this child.

Your son will be financially responsible for his baby. He will be expected to pay child support to the baby's mother from the very beginning. If the baby receives any state or federal money, the father will be held responsible to repay the government for any funds that were used. At parents' nights, I have parents who are attorneys tell me over and over again to warn the boys about their legal, financial responsibility. Attorneys have told me about teen dads who have liens on their houses for $60,000 in money owed to the federal government for health care for a child he fathered 18 years earlier. I've heard of young men who can't get scholarships from colleges or secure a loan for college or even a car because of money owed to the state or federal government for the care of their child. Dads used to be able to get away with not meeting their paternal responsibility, but no more! This is best for the baby and for the dad; no one benefits from a father who shirks his responsibilities. Technology provides tracking mechanisms for men who owe money. It is harder and harder, thank goodness, for him not to fulfill his obligation to his child. This should make your son think seriously about how important those few minutes of sexual thrill can be. Is it worth paying these consequences for the rest of his life?

Raising a child at home has its challenges, but it is still preferred to the alternative. Unfortunately, it is much more common for teens to be pushed out of their family home during the worst crisis they've ever faced. These young parents are on their own, broken up, trying to manage school, finances, housing, childcare, legal fees for custody and child support, and must feed themselves, cloth themselves and attempt to have some semblance of a life. This is an enormously difficult task that brings even the strongest, most independent teens to their knees. It is difficult to overcome the disadvantage of having and raising a baby as a teen.

For an exercise to bring home to your middle or high schooler the financial reality of raising a child , go through the newspapers to look at the costs for her to raise a child on her own (which is the most common scenario). For a list of all the household expenses that are necessary, please see the homework section in the leader's guide for the video series *Sex as God's Gift*, page 21.

When I managed the teen pregnancy project, I found that housing was the greatest challenge. Our teen parents were transient, moving from friend to friend or cheap apartment to cheap apartment. This required all of their energy and time. The girls had a very hard time focusing on anything but the very basics of day-to-day living, food and shelter, and they had very contentious relationships with the fathers of their babies. They needed a lot of community support and used many community resources but continued to have substandard living situations.

Once the pregnancy takes place, the young mom's life is changed. She cannot undo the problem and walk away. The best option is not to get pregnant in the first place. Intercourse makes babies. The only way to be sure pregnancy doesn't happen is to not have intercourse when you cannot support a baby together!

*Option 2: Complete the pregnancy and release the baby
for adoption.*

This is the least commonly used option by teens today. Many of the children I see express that they couldn't imagine "giving their baby up" to someone else. Yet these same children would be more comfortable having an abortion, ending the life of that same baby. Again, that fantastical thinking of adolescence. While no option is perfect, in my opinion, adoption is the best option for teens. If you are not in a position in which pregnancy is acceptable or even feasible, or in which the child's well-being may be maintained, then adoption appears to be the option that does the least harm. Harm is still done, and the young mom will grieve over her baby, some for a short time, one or two years, some for the rest of her life. Some teen moms find that identified adoption helps with grief. Many teen moms who participate in identified adoption keep in contact with the adoptive parents for one to two years and then are able to move on to the next phase of their lives. But her baby will always be part of her life experience. If you read Ann Landers you know how common is the "I want to find my mother" or the "I don't want my child to find me" story.

Some children have questions and concerns when they are raised by parents who did not give birth to them. Loving adoptive parents who take a thoughtful approach to their children's questions and concerns are able to help their children fill in the spaces wherever possible and sort through the issues that may crop up over the course of growing up.

Adoption offers the opportunity of life to a baby and the teenage parents. While it is never easy, it does allow all three involved to move forward in a situation that is at least manageable, something that is not possible for many years if the teenager tries to raise her baby up by herself.

An inspirational and heartwarming story of adoption instead of abortion is told in the movie and book *The Missing*

Piece by Lee Ezell. This is the true story of a young woman who was raped as a virgin and became pregnant. She was encouraged by well-meaning friends to have an abortion; but as a new Christian, she was held back from making that decision by Scripture.

> For you created my inmost being; you knit me together in my mother's womb.
> I praise you because I am fearfully and wonderfully made;
> Your works are wonderful. I know that full well.
> My frame was not hidden from you when I was made in the secret place. When I was woven together in the depths of the earth, your eyes saw my unformed body.
> All the days ordained for me were written in your book before one of them came to be.
>
> Psalm 139:13-16, NIV

This Psalm encouraged this young, battered, emotionally bruised young woman to consider that God could make good out of evil; and she was willing to be the vessel for Him to do that. God did not let Lee Ezell down. She released her baby girl for adoption (the only child she would ever give birth to). She later met and married a young widower with two little daughters whom Lee adopted as her own, and she eventually was united with her beautiful birth daughter, her husband and grandchildren— all servants of the Lord.

While Lee certainly suffered over her decision to carry the baby (she was kicked out of her house by her alcoholic, abusive mother), she also allowed God to turn her suffering into joy. If she had aborted her baby, her suffering would be never-ending. The life of her baby would have been ended, and God's will in her life would have been altered or delayed as a result of her "choice." The third option, the choice for abortion, leaves no choice at all.

Option 3: Abortion

We live in a culture that calls abortion a choice, not the taking of a life. It is no wonder so many teens and sadly, their parents view abortion as a solution to a messy problem—a teen pregnancy. I am continually disheartened at the number of parents who respond to their child's question about what would they do if their child became pregnant by saying, "Abortion, of course." Abortion does not end the problem of a pregnancy; it just ends the pregnancy. The problem of the pregnancy does not go away. It is common for women of any age to have months of "baby" dreams after an abortion. It is common for teens to grieve so much after an abortion that more than 40% of teens who experience abortion are pregnant again in six months, trying to fill the empty space the abortion left behind.

In many states, it is legal for your child to have an abortion without your knowledge. If you have ever filled out the paperwork so that the school nurse can give your child an aspirin, you would be interested to know that the same school nurse very well may be able to arrange for your daughter to have an abortion, even arrange the transportation to the abortion clinic. Yet it is against the law for her to tell the parents without the daughter's permission.

When my seventeen-year-old son drove himself to the doctor's for an appointment for a sore throat, I received a call from the office telling me they would not treat him without me there to sign the form. If my seventeen-year-old daughter went to the doctors to have an abortion, the doctor would perform the abortion without my knowledge and send her home to me that same day without ever contacting me and informing me what my child was going through.

The easiest way to prevent this trouble is by having open, ongoing communication with your children so that they would not feel compelled to keep important life-and-death secrets. But even with great communication and a strong feeling of closeness by the parents, some daughters still can't bring themselves to admit their sexual activity. So they will experience the trauma and heartbreak of abortion alone without the love and advice of the people who love her more than anything.

Abortion ends the life of the baby—your grandchild—and is irreconcilable: there is no going back once the abortion takes place. This inability to rethink her decision, to change her mind and undo the damage, fuels the grief our daughters experience. Our sons have no legal say in the matter of whether the baby is aborted or not; they do not have a choice. It is all up to the teenage mother, and she may do it all alone, only telling her very best friend who swears to keep it a secret. This is a tragedy that happens every day in every community in our country. Helping our children make the decision to wait to have sex is the only way to change the heartbreaking frequency of the choice to abort.

As you can see, once a pregnancy occurs, life is complicated. There are no easy answers for our sons, our daughters or ourselves. The baby is the ultimate victim in a teen pregnancy. The joys of this new baby's birth, along with the dreams and hopes for this new family's future together, are eclipsed when the young parents are unmarried and unprepared to take on the responsibilities of their own lives, never mind the responsibility of a completely dependent baby. All three, both parents and the baby, are starting off with an uphill struggle with money, schooling, their relationship and their parents. This is far from the ideal way to start your family.

Other Factors

Our children have other matters to consider when making the decision about sexual activity. Not only do they have worries about disease, pregnancy, parents, finances, what their friends will think, but they also have to worry about their reputation, both boys and girls, and contraception.

Contraception has been marketed to our children with vigor. If you read the ads for hormonal contraception, "the pill," in any women's magazine, you could easily believe that not only is it healthy for a young woman to take the pill, but it is good for her skin to boot. Hormonal contraceptions are the **pill** (taken once a day), **depoprovera**, (a once-every-three-month injection), and **norplant**, (a long- term implant under the skin of the upper arm that provides five years of hormonal contraception). This form of birth control does not provide protection in any way against sexually transmitted disease. They are the most effective form of pregnancy prevention, **depoprovera** and **norplant** being more effective than birth control pills because the woman does not have to remember to take them.

Hormonal birth control prevents pregnancy in two ways. First, the hormones replicate the hormones of pregnancy, thus suppressing ovulation. Second, the hormones prevent a fertilized egg from being implanted into the uterus by making the uterus a hostile environment for the egg. We should not assume this will not be harmful for our daughters' growing bodies. During adolescence, our daughters' bodies are changing very rapidly. Her reproductive tract is the most vulnerable it will ever be throughout her life. She is at the highest risk for complications from sexually transmitted disease; she will not be finished with puberty for several more years. Hormonal contraception will not protect our daughters from anything but pregnancy, and the cost of that protection over the long term is probably much higher than a teenager should ever pay. Hormonal contraception won't protect our daughters' heart, soul or spirit at all.

Barrier methods of contraception include the condom, diaphragm, and sponge. These methods work by preventing the sperm from meeting the egg. Condoms get a lot of press as the answer to the epidemic of HIV that the world is experiencing. There may be situations in which condoms are the only answer in decreasing the likelihood of transmission of

HIV. If an individual is determined to be sexually active no matter what, then condoms will at least decrease *some* risk of transmission of HIV. But they will do nothing against HPV and chlamydia. Because of all the press condoms have received in light of the HIV epidemic, our children believe they are 98-99% effective in preventing the spread of all STD's. This is flawed information. Condoms, used consistently and correctly, prevent pregnancy less than 80% of the time. Unlike disease, which can be spread every day, pregnancy can occur only the 72 hours a month around the time of ovulation. So logic tells us condoms cannot be more effective than 80% against disease.

When I see high school students I have never seen before and I tell them the truth about contraception, they are generally unwilling to believe me, particularly if they are already sexually active. It is within our human nature to believe that the consequences won't happen to us. They will happen to someone else who is less careful, less in love, not as smart.

Even with the false belief that contraception will prevent any problems as a result of sexual activity, teens as a rule do not use any form of contraception consistently or effectively. The unrealistic thinking of adolescence allows teenagers to think of themselves as "safe" if they use contraception sometimes or even not at all. They assume their safety because they have not had a consequence themselves or because they don't know anyone who has had a consequence. (Remember that the children don't know they have the STD's because most of STD's are symptomless.)

When we look at the ongoing arguments regarding teaching children to use condoms and practice "safe sex," it helps us to understand that we are asking children for a change in behavior to wait to have sex or to use contraception. Either one of these choices is asking our children to change their current behavior. Which choice would you rather your child make: to change her behavior and continue to have risk of pregnancy, disease, heartache and spiritual peril or to change his behavior and have no risk at all? The answer appears clear to me: that my children may make choices that will not cause permanent harm, physically, emotionally or spiritually.

Where God Fits In

Let's try to get a clear picture of the gift of sexuality. Intercourse is a gift from God. He has given us a great gift in allowing us to share in the miracle of creation. God's job is new life, and He gives to us, generously and fully, the opportunity to share in creation through intercourse. This is a gift we must take seriously. God has loved us enough to give us this great gift, though we disobey Him and go our own way and even ignore Him unless we need Him. Think of your new baby's face, how your heart filled with love as you looked at your beautiful infant. Think of how you didn't even know what love was until you held your first baby in your arms and how you didn't know your capacity for love until you held your last child there.

I tell the children to think of their favorite person, someone whom they love a lot. This person's birthday is coming up and you want to show him how important he is to you. You want to give him the best gift possible. So you think and think and finally decide to buy a portable CD player because this friend loves music and is always on the go. The gift is expensive and is very valuable, so you have to save your money to afford it. While you are saving up, you are imagining your friend listening to his favorite music and enjoying his gift. You finally have enough money to buy the gift. You go to his birthday party and see that this friend is getting a lot of great gifts. He opens them all one at a time, is very polite, says thank you to everyone, and piles his gifts up on the floor around his chair. You are so excited when he gets to yours because you really think you have the best gift. He loves your present!! He says, "Thank you so much. I love it," and he puts it on the floor in front of him while he finishes opening his gifts. Once all the gifts are open and your friend is saying "thank you, thank you" to everyone, he stands up and he STEPS on your gift. He just smashes it right into the ground, saying "thank you" all the while, loving the sound the CD player makes as it cracks and breaks against the floor. How do you feel about that? The children are usually outraged.

I ask them to think of how God must feel. He thought and thought about His creation and chose as one of many gifts the ability to participate in creation, to make new life. We love this gift. We like the way it makes us feel, the closeness it brings us with another person. We like everything about it—almost. The "new life" part is pretty inconvenient in today's world. In our culture we take this very valuable gift of making new life and turn it into something worthless, just like our friend with the CD player. We say "thank you" for the gift and then use it in a way it was never intended. We use the gift of sexuality in a way that brings harm in the form of disease, unintended pregnancy, and conflict between parent and child. Our culture uses the gift of sexuality to sell cars and beer. We as Christians know differently. New life is an incredible gift. We need to revere the act that allows that to happen.

Pray for and with your child regarding the decision to be sexually active. Start praying about this in middle school. In your prayers, recognize temptation and ask God to be there with your child whenever temptation occurs. Maggie and I pray about Maggie's and Steve's future spouses. We pray that they are being raised up in the way they should go. We pray that they are getting to know God. We pray that they are making good decisions, the same good decisions Maggie will be making and that Steve already makes. We pray that God is keeping them close and watching over them carefully.

Share this chapter with your child, read about the risks together and have a conversation. We can influence the choices our children make in their relationships. The choice is ultimately our child's to make; we cannot make it for them. But we can provide enough prayer, information, love and structure to help our teen make the decision to wait to be sexually active.

Things to Think About

- What are your opinions on premarital sex?
- Have you had a conversation with your child about sex? Not the mechanics but the heart, commitment and relationship aspects? If not, could you?
- Do you know God's desires for us sexually?
- Do you know if your child is planning on waiting to be sexually active?
- Do you make decisions that emphasize long-term rewards?
- Do you discuss the benefits of waiting (for anything) with your child?
- Do you allow the decisions you made for yourself when you were young interfere with your starting the conversation about waiting for sex with your child?
- Do you have rules about dating? Should you?
- Do you feel guilty about past decisions of your own?

Things to Do

- Pray for your child specifically about his decision regarding sexual activity outside of marriage.
- Pray about your past decisions about sexual activity and any of the consequences you have experienced. Ask God for forgiveness, and let Him forgive. (Easier said than done. We often prefer to hold on to the guilt, but it is much better for everyone if you let God do His work in you.)
- Pray with your child for her future spouse, that he is being raised up in the way he should go, that he is making the same good decisions your child is making, and that God is keeping him in His tender loving care.

- Talk with your child about emotional health, communication with people you care about, and handling the strong feelings of sexual desire.
- Talk to your child about relationships, long versus short. Emphasize the value of long-term relationships.
- Talk to your child about commitment and what forever means.
- Read this chapter together; discuss the consequences.
- Establish guidelines for dating for your teenager. See chapter 7 on waiting for ideas.
- Show your child affection; express your love in words and hugs, pats on the back and goodnight kisses.

Scripture to Remember

- James 1:12 - Blessed is the man who endures temptation.
- James 1:14 - Each one is tempted when he is drawn away by his own desires.
- Romans 12:1 - Present your bodies a living sacrifice, holy, acceptable to God.
- 1 Corinthians 13:4-8 (NIV) - Love is patient and is kind. It does not envy, it does not boast, it is not proud. It is not rude, it is not self-seeking, it is not easily angered.... It always protects, always trusts, always hopes, always perseveres.
- 1 Corinthians 10:13 - No temptation has overtaken you except such as is common to man; but God is faithful, who will not allow you to be tempted beyond what you are able, but with temptation will also make the way of escape so that you will be able to bear it.
- 1 Thessalonians 4:3 (NIV) - It is God's will that you should be sanctified: that you should avoid sexual immorality; that each of you should learn to control his own body.
- 2 Timothy 2:21-22 - Flee also youthful lusts; but pursue righteousness, faith, love, peace with those who call on the Lord out of a pure heart.

- Psalm 139:13-16 (NIV)
  For you created my inmost being; you knit me together
  in my mother's womb.
  I praise you because I am fearfully and wonderfully
  made;
  Your works are wonderful. I know that full well.
  My frame was not hidden from you when I was made in
  the secret place. When I was woven together in the
  depths of the earth, your eyes saw my unformed
  body.
  All the days ordained for me were written in your book
  before one of them came to be.

Children who have to entertain themselves, think up games to play, make up a story and follow it through to the end, and rely on themselves for entertainment (rather than simply being entertained, especially by TV) will have an easier time sitting and paying attention in school from the earliest grades.

9

POPULAR Culture's Influence

Imagine that we came to school this morning and our principal told us to go home, pack our suitcases and come back to catch the bus for a trip to the beach. We are very excited, so we run home as fast as we can, pack our stuff and head off to the beach! We have the best time we've ever had. We swim, lay on the beach, play volleyball, just have a great time. While we are there, all day every day, the waves come up to the shore, take a few grains of sand and bring the sand back out to the ocean. We are completely unaware of this happening as we enjoy ourselves. When the week is over we promise to have a reunion back at the same beach in ten years, and we all go home. During the ten years that we are gone, no one does anything to save the beach. All day every day the waves wash up onto the shore. There is an occasional storm that washes away some extra sand every now and then, and no one does anything to stop it. No one keeps the jetties built up, no one plants sea grass along the dunes, no one puts up signs that tell us not to walk on the dunes, and no one erects any fencing.

When we return to the beach for our ten year reunion we find a very different beach. The erosion that has taken place has changed the character and nature of the beach we visited. And it changed it one grain of sand at a time while no one was paying any attention, while no one was taking action to preserve the beauty and unspoiled character of our beautiful place. The changes occurred while we were having fun, enjoying the pleasures of the beach, without ever giving a thought to how many changes were taking place.

Anyone who has ever given seminars to middle school students will tell you the importance of breaking the ice with them right away. The activity I started using ten years ago with the children has turned into one of the most interesting fact-gathering activities I do with each new group of students.

Each program I give begins with the students' answering questions about how they spend their time. I ask them to respond by raising their hands to questions about TV, movies, video games, music, favorite magazines, extracurricular activities and their families. Following are examples of the questions asked. For a full listing of the questions please see the Appendix A on page 217.

About Television

- How many of you watch TV every day?
- How many of you have TV's in your bedroom?

About Movies

- How many of you have seen at least two R-rated movies in the past two months?
- How many of you have rules about movies? Based on content? Ratings? Other information your parents might have (e.g., if they have seen it themselves, heard something or read reviews)?

About Video Games

- How many of you like to play video games?
- How many of you play video games every day?
- How many of you have played your video games with your parents?

About Magazines

- How many of you like to read magazines?

About Music

- How many of you listen to more music than you watch TV?
- How many of you prefer to watch your music (music videos)?
- How many of your parents have ever read the lyrics to your music?

About Extracurricular Activities

- How many of you stay after school at least three days per week for something other than detention?
- How many of you go out to lessons or meetings in the evening at least two nights per week?

About Family

- How many of you are the oldest child?
- How many of you are the youngest?
- How many of you eat dinner with at least some of your family most nights?

When I first started asking these questions, I asked fewer questions, simply about TV, movies and extracurricular activities. But over the past ten years the questions have expanded as a result of the answers I receive from the thousands of students I see every year. As the students answered some of my questions, it brought more questions to mind. Sometimes the students would tell me a question I ought to be asking. Several students brought to mind that I ought to ask about stepfamilies and who the children live with. Some of the questions are asked only to certain age groups. (I don't ask high school seniors about the rules about TV, movies and video games.) I'd like to share with you some of the results from this informal, unscientific research.

About Television

Most of the students I see watch TV, lots of it, as a matter of fact. The most TV watching seems to take place between fifth and ninth grades. It is common for the high school children to have so much going on that they don't have time for TV. So although most high school students are daily watchers, they spend fewer hours per week in front of the screen.

In any given group of middle school students, at least 70% of the class watches TV for at least 3 hours per day. At first, though, they don't think so. But once they realize it is only 3 one-hour shows per day, or 1 hour in the morning and a couple of hours in the evening, more hands go up. Most of us are unaware of the true amount of time we spend in front of the TV. Our children are no exception.

Most of the students have TV's in their bedrooms. More children in communities of poverty have TV's in their bedrooms than in middle class communities, and more children in wealthy communities have TV's in their bedrooms than middle class children as well. I worry about all the children with TV's in their bedrooms. They can watch as much of any kind of TV they desire without the parents' having any awareness at all of what is being watched. Watching TV is an isolating experience. Observe any group of people watching a show other than sports, and you will see very little interaction between the members of the group. If someone talks, everyone else shushes him. Watching TV alone in your room is even more isolating; there isn't even someone sharing the experience with you.

It is hard for me to imagine a lonelier family picture than everyone off in their own bedrooms, watching their own shows for the entire evening after a dinner spent with the TV on. There is no dialogue, no bonding, and no opportunity to get to know one another better. It is not uncommon for us to know more about a celebrity than we know about a member of our own family.

According to an organization called TV-free America, the average American teen watches 3 hours of TV per day. The same teen spends 15 minutes talking to mom and 7 minutes talking to dad.[1] This begs the question of who has more influence over that teenager?

The numbers are staggering: the average American middle school child spends more than 20 hours per week in front of the television.[2] Studies show that if a child watches more than 10 hours of TV per week, academic performance will be impaired. At the end of the average lifespan, an average person will have watched more than ten uninterrupted years of TV, more than hours spent on hobbies, time with family or going to school all the way through graduate school! The average middle school student will spend 1,600 hours watching TV during the year and 900 hours in school. **By age five, a child will have spent more time watching TV than he will spend talking to his father his whole life.**[3]

How could we begin to imagine that this much TV watching won't influence the way our children feel, think and act? Our children are watching misbehaving, out of control, rude, disobedient, outrageous behavior on their favorite television shows from a very young age. Much of television that is marketed to our youngsters shows homes in which children are in charge, not the parents. One parent is deceased or has disappeared, and the other is out of control, or the parents are divorced and more worried about their love lives than about their children. The young adults portrayed on popular TV are wildly promiscuous, live a lifestyle they would never be able to afford in light of their job situation and have no respect for themselves, never mind for anyone else. The shows for our sons are very violent. Even if it is "fake," it is violent. Watch less than five minutes of World Wrestling Federation, and you will see exactly what I mean. A study published in the January, 2001, *Archives of Pediatrics and Adolescent Medicine* identified a direct link between watching TV and playing video games and patterns of aggression in third and fourth graders. They found that students who had reduced video games and TV to seven hours per week or less had about half as many playground incidents of verbal aggression compared to the students who did not cut back. They also found a 25% reduction in the reports of aggressive behavior among their peers.[4]

If television didn't change the way we think and act, advertising wouldn't be so expensive. Why else would companies be willing to spend millions of dollars on TV advertising if it didn't change spending habits—especially children's? The job of advertising is to get us to want what we don't have or to feel that what we have is inadequate, so that we want more.

The tenth commandment warns us not to want what isn't ours. It tells us not to want different houses, people or possessions in our lives. Could God be warning us against wanting what isn't ours because it makes us dissatisfied? I know that I have the least joy, peace and goodwill in my life when I am wanting something I can't afford or shouldn't have. Advertising puts us in a position of constant temptation to want what isn't ours. Each commercial, each show, gives us a glimpse of something we don't have yet. It is difficult to have gratitude for the abundance in our lives if we are constantly exposed to what we lack.

My family understands the power of advertising, having stopped watching TV for a number of years when our children were small, about four and nine. We didn't stop watching for any high-minded ideals. We stopped watching because we were having construction on our house, and the only TV we owned was in the room where the construction was taking place. There was no furniture in this room anymore.

Everything was covered in dust, and it was cold in there. But every night I went in, sat on the floor and got my "fix." One night my husband told me to give it up and find something better to do with my time. I took his advice, more out of embarrassment about my habit than anything else. We stopped watching TV, moved it out of the house and became a TV-free family.

I noticed some changes almost right away. When we went grocery shopping, I didn't have to fight with them over the types of cereals we bought. When Christmas came, the children had very small lists; they actually didn't know what they wanted. We learned how to spend our time together talking, playing games, reading out loud–habits that continued for many years. We found out that we really liked each other and enjoyed spending time together. So we began to spend our time together in more meaningful ways.

I'm sorry to report that we eventually did acquire another TV that we keep hidden in a cabinet so that it is not an ever-present reminder to turn it on. I have become the anti-TV person in the household. We continue to spend most of our time together TV-free. Our TV is on for fewer than 2 hours a day, always after 9:00 p.m., and we watch no network TV. But to tell you the truth, I'm not happy that we have one at all, even though I watch. Maggie, a young teen, does not watch TV at all; she has no interest. She wouldn't know what was on or when it was on. She is not in on all the TV conversation at school, and she truly doesn't care. She seems to have plenty of friends who like her anyway. She'd rather read, play games, and practice her dancing or piano. I believe this is from her very early years of not developing the habit. It continues to this day. The advantage is all hers (and ours).

If, like most of us, you have a TV, I suggest developing some structure around the amount of time watching and the content that is watched. It is unusual for a middle school student to raise her hand in answer to the question about rules for TV. While I understand that some children just don't want to admit they have rules, that can't possibly account for the absence of rules about TV for middle school students that I see. In some Catholic elementary schools, I find middle school students who can't watch TV until their homework is done or who have limits on the time or type of shows they can watch. But this is the exception rather than the rule. We can change this; we should change this. Parents have the ability to influence the viewing and game-playing habits of their children.

Even if you have never had any guidelines about TV, it is never too late to start. While most families would have difficulty in cutting the cord completely, it is well advised to decrease the amount of time your children spend watching TV instead of doing other activities. Here are some suggestions to get you started.

(1) Start by keeping a log of what is watched and when.

Each person in the family should keep his own log. Each time the TV is on, whoever is watching has to record what they are watching and for how long. Even if you are just channel surfing, write it down. You will be amazed at how much of your most precious resource, time, is used in front of the TV.

(2) Remove all TV's from the house except for one in the room where the family spends the most time.

Parents can keep a TV in their room, but be aware that a bedroom TV is harmful to your sex life.

(3) Ask your children what their favorite show is and watch it together.

Decide if this is appropriate viewing for your child. If you don't think so, discuss the show and your feelings with your child at a later date, in a calm fashion. Make a rule: no more watching this show; or, you can watch this show only if I watch it with you, or something along those lines.

(4) Decide on an appropriate amount of TV time per child, and enforce it.

You can do this in any way that works for your family, but here are a couple of suggestions from parents: When the TV guide arrives, have each child look through it and choose either a limited number of shows or limited amount of time for the week. They have to stick to what they chose even if something "better" comes along during the week. The children have to negotiate with each other if they want to watch something at the same time. This option not only decreases TV time; but it also teaches planning, prioritizing, negotiation and compromise. If the children get fighting over what to watch, no one gets to watch anything. Another suggestion is very effective if your children are small. *Give them a certain number of tokens for a week; each token equals one half hour of TV.* You decide how much is appropriate, maybe two hours per week. Each time your child watches a show, she gives you a token until the tokens are used up. This teaches planning skills, prioritizing and long-term thinking. If they use up all the tokens by Tuesday, it could become a very long week. It usually doesn't take too many long weeks for a child to start to ration her TV time and watch only something really favored.

(5) Begin a "no surfing" rule (after your log is finished).

Flipping through the channels wastes time and fills our children's heads with visions of sex, violence and glorification of the lowest possible levels of humanity. What are you looking for? Before you know it, you have used up an hour looking for something worth watching, and you have watched small amounts of lots of invaluable programming and commercials.

To learn what your child watches when he is flipping through, try the following. Flip through your channels and stop at the most popular channels—Fox, the WB, MTV, USA, Comedy Central, the WWF channel and any other channel you know your child enjoys. Spend enough time on each to watch the show and commercials; on sports channels you can just watch the commercials. Do you like what you've seen? If not, remember you are the parent. It is up to you to decide how the resources of your household will be used. Only planned shows should be watched. If you don't know of something specific on that you want to see, leave the TV off. Do something else instead.

We should not view TV as harmless recreation. It influences our thinking and reinforces faulty information. Despite the incredible promiscuity among the young and hip on TV, no one ever gets an STD. You can turn the TV on at any time of the day and see unmarried people having sex with each other without any consequences or with consequences that are somehow magically resolved within a 30-minute time-frame.

The children tell me they know TV isn't real, that it is just for entertainment, only fun. Do you remember educational toys? How many of these did you buy for your child when he was small? Did we think they would learn more easily or more readily if they were just having fun? Of course we did, or we wouldn't have bought them. One prominent toy catalog has the slogan, "Children learn best when they are having fun." TV is fun. And it is this "fun" that reinforces television's messages and themes in children's minds. But I am surprised at how many high school aged students get the reality/fantasy issue mixed up. When I talk with high school students about some of the consequences of sexual activity, there is invariably at least one student in every class who will use a TV show as an example to refute my statistics. The student will say, "But on 'Jerry Springer'. . . ," or "On 'Friends'. . . ." So while they understand intellectually that TV is fake, in their hearts, as they watch, they absorb the information as if it is true.

There is a saying: If you put a frog in a pot of boiling water he will jump right out; if you put a frog in a pot of room-temperature water, then raise the temperature one degree at a time, you will cook him.

This is what is happening with television today. When I was growing up in the 1970's, my favorite shows were "I Love Lucy," "Petticoat Junction," "Green Acres" and "The Brady Bunch." Lucy and Ricky had twin beds, and THEY WERE MARRIED! Petticoat Junction, if written today, probably would be something dirty instead of the "oh, gosh" kind of humor that it had. TV was very different. We've moved from Lucy and Ricky Ricardo's twin beds to "The Howard Stern Show," showing naked women, ogled by dysfunctional men. We didn't get there in one big leap. We moved to "Laugh-in," "Dallas," "Charlie's Angels," "Dynasty," one step at a time, up to one of the popular shows for teenagers, believe it or not, "Howard Stern."

Even shows that parents feel comfortable with, like the currently popular "Seventh Heaven," have teens that are sleeping around, having abortions, drinking until they are sick, and using drugs as if all young people do this. Although there is a moral to the story, the message that these behaviors are so commonplace, that "everyone is doing it," sticks with our children. This adds to the already significant pressure our children feel from their friends and from their own desires.

Choose to be conscious consumers of what television has to offer. Use your parental authority to make decisions about acceptable and unacceptable forms of entertainment, and let your child know the reasons for your decisions. You may have to start with, "This may come as a surprise to you since we haven't had many rules before. I have learned something new about TV: It is very influential in our culture, and we believe that much of that influence is negative. I now understand how important it is for you that I make these decisions. I don't expect you to love these new rules, but I do expect you to obey them."

About Movies

It is disheartening to learn how many middle school students watch R-rated movies. The greatest majority of sixth grade students I see report watching R-rated movies. Some of these students are watching with their own parents, some with parents of friends, some with an older brother, sister or friend.

Movies today are not like movies when we were growing up. When I was in middle school, Midnight Cowboy was released. It was rated X when it was first released. I remember my parents' discussing what was going wrong with the world when movies like this were being made. What was so objectionable? Sex with a prostitute. Such is now included in so-called "family-friendly" movies like the ever-popular "Forrest Gump." Like TV, movies have changed in the frog-in-the-pot way, a little at a time so that we hardly notice it happening.

As with television, few children seem to have rules about movies. Some of the younger students, fifth and sixth grade, tell me their parents need either to see the movie first or watch it with them, maybe fast-forwarding through objectionable parts. This is certainly better than having the children watch the movie alone or with friends because the parents provide a bit of a filter. It is not, however, a *great* idea. We are watching the movie with the life experience of 30 or 40 years, and our children are watching with the life experience and limited development of a 10 or 12 year old. Many parts of 10- to 12-year-old thinking are still concrete. They cannot yet view an event abstractly. They are still at an age when they take things at face value. They will process what they watch differently from how we will. It is as much about physical development as social and emotional experience.

Movies are rated for a reason. The intent behind the ratings is to protect your child from being exposed to material that is inappropriate. Hollywood is not a very conservative place. If they say you ought to be seventeen to see a movie, you probably ought to be twenty, certainly not twelve.

If you read the papers or news magazines, if you follow politics at all, you may have developed an opinion on whether or not it is important to limit Hollywood. If you believe this should be done, the truth is that it is not up to our politicians or the media or even Hollywood to make the changes. It is up to *us*, within the context of our family. The best way to limit Hollywood is with our dollars. The movie industry, like any other, is in business to make money. As long as our dollars support garbage, garbage will continue to be made. The only way to make a difference is not to see the movies that are objectionable. When Hollywood says they only make what sells, they are right. The question I have is how can we as parents allow them to sell what they make to our children? Why should the government have to tell us as parents that R-rated movies shouldn't be seen by a twelve year old? We should know this! We have within our control the ability to make a difference.

We have to act on what is right for our child without making decisions based on our child's popularity. Use your parental authority to decide what movies your child should and shouldn't see. Please use the ratings as a minimum guideline only. If the industry tells us you must be thirteen, wait *at least* until your child is thirteen. If the industry says seventeen, wait at least until then. Your child will learn how to wait; he will learn the truth about sometimes standing alone when you do what is right. As a result, he will miss the pollution of his mind that the movies will provide.

Let us remember as parents that our job is not to make our child conform to what is popular, but to teach our child to make decisions for what is right. If we worry about our child's popularity, and we use that as a consideration for our decision-making about our child, we are doing him a tremendous disservice.

When my son Steve was in fifth grade, he was invited to a sleepover at one of his classmates. In his school, there is only one class for each grade, and all the boys from his class were invited to the party. He came home and told me about the invitation and in the same breath told me I probably wasn't going to let him go because they were going to watch an R-rated movie. He was eleven—they all were—and this mother was going to show them a movie that was meant for an adult audience. So I started to call other mothers to see if they were going to let their son go. I thought I knew which mothers would object and which wouldn't, and I began calling the moms I thought felt as I did. I was wrong. All the other moms decided to send their child because the movie "wasn't that bad"—there wasn't any sex, just "action" (another term for shooting, bombing, car wrecks, lots of death and destruction). While making those calls, I realized I was showing my son that other people's opinions were more important than sticking to our principles. This was not the message I wanted to send.

I put the phone down and told him I was sorry that he couldn't go to the party. I told him I felt so bad that the mother giving the party put me in the position in which he had to miss the party. I told him that anything that he wanted to do the night of the party we would do as a family. Anything. That started a family tradition. If we had to say "no," whoever we said it to could pick something fun to do, and the family would do it. Sometimes we'd go out to dinner, go shopping, rent a movie, or have pizza. It got us through those challenging years of middle school. We had a lot of fun as a family in the process.

Maggie is now a middle school student. As a result of our approach with Stephen, she usually doesn't even ask us to do things we wouldn't approve of. She watched and learned how our family operates from the great advantage of being the second child. It has been easier for her because she knows how far to push, she understands the limits, and she trusts that we will not change our basic beliefs: what was true for her brother will also be true for her. I'm confident that Maggie would push us further, want more privileges and feel more pressure to conform to popular culture if we had taken a different approach with her brother.

We are changed by what we watch through a process very similar to erosion. When I explain to the children why it is best not to watch many movies, certainly movies that are rated for older viewers, or spend too much time in front of the TV, I describe the process as in the story at the beginning of this chapter. This is the manner in which our popular culture changes our children. It alters the way they think, feel and act one small step at a time. We don't see the changes as we live with our children, when the day-to-day needs of the family are our priority. But the changes are occurring. It is our job as the parents to establish the safety measures to allow our children to grow into the people God desires them to be, not the people our popular culture will shape them into being. One of these measures needs to be the guidelines we establish for exposure to movies, television, music, magazines and other popular culture influences.

About Video Games

Video games are to parents of the new century what drugs were to parents of the sixties and seventies. We are not informed enough to make good decisions. I had admit my ignorance, since we don't have these in our home, until a group of sixth grade boys in a Christian school started talking about their favorite video games. They enthusiastically told me the names of their favorite games, how they were played, and which parts were their favorites. I could not believe the steps necessary to move from one level to another to win. I was so surprised at the casual way they discussed shooting, blowing up and stabbing people.

153

These students took me by surprise.

They talked about games in which you get another life by killing someone. They talked about one of their favorite games because you don't lose points for killing innocent bystanders. The very favorite required that they kill a monk and the screen would go red with blood in order to win. They enjoyed a game in which they killed from cars, were awarded condoms as points, and could shoot at people through metal stairs and watch them die from below.

These were nice children in a nice school in a nice town being raised by nice parents. They played these games every day; sometimes their parents played with them. After this visit I started to ask about video games, and I found that these sixth graders were typical. How can this form of recreation be harmless? How can our children spend their leisure time shooting, killing, being reborn and killing again in bloody graphic detail without having their thinking affected? Clearly, we have seen too many situations of mass shooting in public places and student-to-student massacres in schools across the country to believe these games don't affect their thinking.

Video games are very expensive, and they seem to be a totally unproductive use of time. Students who play video games are more likely to be obese, develop type 2 diabetes and demonstrate aggressive behavior towards others.[5] In my opinion, they would be better off using up their aggressions in the backyard or on their bike. If they have to relax, they should read a book instead of blowing someone up.

Do you know what games your children play? Do you play with them? Are they violent? Do you pay attention to the ratings? Like the movies, the ratings are there for a reason. "M" means mature audience—adults over seventeen. The ratings are on the front of the box. Do your homework. Go to a video and computer game store, and spend an hour or so looking at the video games that are marketed to your children. Do you like what you see? If not, make decisions about what games your child may or may not play. Use your parental authority to let your children know why you don't want them to play certain games, and stick to it. Make conscious choices about how you spend your time together. Instead of playing a video game together, how about shooting some baskets or going for a walk or riding your bikes together? Go outside at night to look at the stars, stand in the garage to watch it rain, develop a hobby together, build something. You could read a book together and talk about it, learn how to develop your own pictures, wrestle, play a board game, or play cards. You'll talk to each other more, and all of these activities would promote family bonding and communication through positive activities. You have less control over what they do when they are not in your house. You *can* control how the resources of your family are spent. Do it.

About Magazines

Magazines are truly the "frog in the pot." When I was a young mother, I enjoyed *Redbook* magazine. They had fiction, recipes, ideas about parties, a little bit of decorating and fashion. It was a very enjoyable magazine. Now the cover of every *Redbook* has two feature stories, one about sex and one about weight loss, every month. One feature is called "REDHOT sex." No doubt about it. *Redbook* has changed, and *Redbook* is not alone. Look at any women's magazine, and you will find the emphasis is very much on sex and appearance. The next time you are in the grocery store or pharmacy, take a minute to read the covers of the magazines at the checkout. Even if you don't read the tabloids, you will find most cover stories relate to being thin and having sex. These must be the only two issues women care about for them to make so many covers of so many magazines the way they do.

This is at its worst in the magazines that are geared toward our teenage daughters. One would think from reading the magazines called *YM, Seventeen, Cosmo Girl* and *Teen People* that the only value our daughters bring to life would be the way they look and what they can do for you. There is very little about success in the ways you would want your daughter to be successful. Little talk of career, kindness, friendship, intelligence, sense of humor, or perseverance. No encouragement for the skills that our daughters need to make their way in this life. Only value for your body: how it looks and what it does. Popular magazines tell our children get the message that sex is more important than any other aspect of their lives. Do you believe this to be true for your life? If not, do you want your daughter to believe this about her life? Or do you desire another healthier perspective for your middle school girl?

If you want something better for your daughter, you are in charge of making the change. Do you purchase the magazines your child reads? If so, choose not to use your family resources to buy materialistic, "obsessed with the physical" reading material. If there is a subscription I suggest you get the mail and read the magazine first. Don't just skim it; read it. Each month if you feel there is a benefit to your daughter's reading the magazine, discuss it with her, clarify any misconceptions she may be developing about body size or the importance of boys or growing up. For me, this took a lot of effort. It was simpler just not to buy the magazines that preach the negative messages for me or Maggie. We seemed to do better without the influence entering the house at all. I preferred that we both read other material.

When choosing magazines for both sons and daughters, encourage their interest with special interest magazines about sports, computers, cars, dance, music, science or whatever your child enjoys. There are several good Christian magazines: *Brio* and *Breakaway* from Focus on the Family and *Campus Life* for high school students are good general reading. Go to a store with a large magazine section. (Bookstores usually have a pretty good selection.) Look over the choices together to see if there are any that might meet your needs. Buy it for a couple of months before you decide to get a subscription, just to be sure.

This may seem like a lot of effort, but the time and energy is worth it if it helps your child take her time going through childhood and have a healthier view of herself and relationships as a result. As with television and movies, we have to be conscious consumers of the media, considering their impact on our child's growing mind.

About Music

Are you familiar with your child's favorite musician? Have you ever read the lyrics of any of your child's CD's? If not, you are not alone. Most of the students I see report that their parents were unfamiliar with the content of their music. The only rules about music that any student at any age seems to have is related to volume, and some children can't play some of their music around a little brother or sister. I've never understood what would be okay for a fifth or sixth grader that wouldn't be okay for a second or third grader.

Students of all ages report that parents do not pay attention to the warning labels. I strongly advise you to do this. Look at the warning label, and read the lyrics before you allow family resources to support an artist or group that expresses thoughts or ideas that you believe are wrong. Rap and heavy metal music are not the only ones at fault. Try reading the lyrics of current female pop stars like Christina Aguilera and Brittany Spears. I'm not sure you are going to like what you read. Your child is listening to this—through headphones so that no other stimuli gets in—for several hours every day. If your child is not listening to the music, she may be watching it, most likely on MTV. Watch for yourself and develop an opinion about what you see. Decide if this is appropriate for your daughters or sons. Decide if this helps them to grow up slowly, enjoy their youth and learn how to build healthy, happy future relationships.

Would watching or listening to this bring your child closer to God or further away? Are you "raising him up in the way he should go" by supporting this artist? Ultimately, these are the questions we have to answer. We can't control every exposure our child has; he will go to other homes and listen to music we think is trash, play video games we wouldn't approve of, and watch TV shows that we don't watch. Small doses of that are okay because you're setting the standard in your household for what you think is right and wrong. Your child will not feel deprived if the standards are set with love and understanding. Your child will feel protected and cared for once she understands that your job is to be sure she grows up with healthy thinking and that you don't believe that particular music, movie, TV show or video game will help her to do that.

Expect resistance if you begin to apply your rules after seventh or eighth grade. That doesn't mean you can't do it; it just means it will be more difficult. With music, just like with TV and movies, we need to be aware of what our child is listening to. Smart parents listen with their children, read the lyrics, talk about the messages and make some decisions about how the family resources are used. This isn't a matter of taste; it is a matter of standards. Some Christian groups contain rap-oriented music, but the message is correct. We have to try to separate what we like or don't like from what we view as right or wrong.

My son liked some bands that I thought for a brief time were questionable during middle school. We made a deal that I was to read the lyrics of all the CD's he bought, and if I thought they were inappropriate he would return them. We had to return one once; he monitored his buying habits after that. I have learned to enjoy Steve's taste in music very much. He actually has more sophisticated taste than I do, but he still needed a little gentle intervention in middle school about the type of thinking we are willing to support as a family.

About Extracurricular Activities

This is the area in which I see the biggest difference from school to school based on economics. The wealthier the community, the more extracurricular activities. In some communities the children do everything; they play sports, play an instrument, dance, participate in theatre, take lessons for everything. They go out most evenings and many afternoons to participate in all the various events. They are exhausted and stressed. They don't have time for religious education, and they take the honors track in school so they have tons of homework to do at the same time. The entire family is running in 10 different directions all the time, grabbing a bite to eat in the car and going from one activity to the next. Home is really just logistics central. Is this you?

I was the speaker at a parent/student night for a large suburban church in early September. The night was to begin the religious education year for students who were going to be confirmed. Before the evening began, I was walking up and down the aisles, handing out pencils and notecards when I was stopped by a mother, way in the back with her fifteen-year-old daughter. She inquired as to how long I was going to talk. She didn't really "have time for this." Her daughter just came from soccer practice (it was 7:30 p.m.) and hadn't been home from school yet. She was exhausted and had homework to do. This mother was furious at her church for scheduling something they both had to be at. (Didn't the church know they were busy? When is the church ever going to learn?)

I was stunned. She didn't complain about the soccer practice that kept her child for many hours. She didn't complain about the 3 hours of homework her child had. She complained about the one hour God-centered, parent/child program which focuses on bringing her child closer to God and helping her make healthy decisions as a result! I know she was not alone in her frustration that night. It concerns me what that says about our priorities.

Somewhere is a fairly happy medium. It is up to each family to find what works for their children. If you feel too busy, you probably are. If you never have time for dinner together, if the children are usually still doing homework late at night because they came home so late from practice, if your child is tired all the time and can't get out of bed in the morning or is often sick, you probably are doing too much. Be sure to leave some pockets of time for reading, taking a hike, going for a bike ride, or shooting some baskets. Everyone needs a little down time; some people need more than others.

If you have a child that wants only down time and is reluctant to get involved in anything, your challenge is to help him find an activity he enjoys. Sometimes we think only of the more common activities like sports or scouts, but some of our children will do better in less common choices. They might enjoy drum corp, volunteering at the library or a nursing home, police explorers, building models, sewing classes, French lessons, bird watching, or learning how to cook. Be creative, look around, and ask at your church, a local volunteer center, or the library. Find out about opportunities to get involved at school and encourage your child. If your child would like to try something new or unfamiliar, give it a try, even if it is something that only "nerds" would have done when you were a child.

I am the student council mom at my children's school. Student council gives the children a chance to practice leadership and role-modeling. They volunteer to help others and to help their school. It's pretty fun. I was with a group of girls and moms just before the student council elections. We were talking about who was running and who wasn't when one mom said to her daughter, "I hope you're not running; that is such a geeky thing to do." Well, in some contexts student council may be *called* "geeky," but why would she discourage her child from doing something that is good and fun? Let's be careful about this. If it is healthy, involves our child constructively, and doesn't interfere with time as a family or with time for church, carefully consider it.

If your children need to be home alone for any reason after school, it is best that you help them to fill those after-school hours as constructively as possible. This is very tough if you have transportation problems. Try to research what is available after school in the building or in the neighborhood or carpooling with another parent. Ask the counselors at school, or look into youth development at your local YMCA or any other youth-serving agency in your community. The three or four hours after school home alone are the highest risk hours of the day. You can help your child fill these hours in a way that is productive, helpful to others, and meaningful to his growth and development. I am not telling you this to put more stress on your already stress-filled situation, but I hope to encourage you to take steps to prevent problems during the teenage years. Supervision is the best prevention. Volunteer programs, athletic activities, and after-school clubs are supervised. They may not feel like they are being watched (and this is best), but they do have adults watching after them all the same.

Standing Alone

Many parents I meet ask me how they can make decisions to limit what movies their child sees when most of their friends are watching them. What can they say to their child? How can they allow their child to be "the only one" who doesn't get to do something? First, let me reassure you that your child will not only *survive* being "the only one," but he also will benefit from it. We all have to know how to stand alone on something that is important. We all have to know how to take an unpopular stand for what is right. How will we know how to do this if we don't practice it? Parents can give their child a chance to practice doing what is right, not just what is popular.

Overview

All forms of entertainment teach us something. It is up to us as parents to decide if we like the messages that our children are learning. Once we make a decision about our preferences, we can develop a support structure that will provide rules and limits for our children with regards to how they spend their leisure time.

Many middle schools divide the students by cluster or level. When I go to these middle schools, I see the students based on the cluster they are in. There is a striking difference in the amount of pop culture exposure between the children in the honors cluster and the children in the learning difficulty cluster. Without exception, at the schools I teach in, the children in the learning difficulty clusters, the children who have the hardest time sitting still, attending to detail, and behaving themselves in class are the same children who see the most TV, watch the most R-rated movies, have the TV's in their bedrooms, and have the fewest parental controls.

Since my survey is anecdotal and unscientific, I can't fairly speculate about this result. I'm not sure if the difficulty sitting and learning comes first so that the TV and movies help to corral the energy, or if it is a result of too much time being entertained and not enough time using the body and brain in a way that helps it to work better.

Michael Medved, in his book *Saving Childhood* believes that the pop culture exposure comes first, and school trouble comes later. The images on TV change every few seconds. Children who watch an abundance of this do not learn how to pay attention because the stimulation is constantly changing. Children who have to entertain themselves think up games to play, make up a story and follow it through to the end, and rely on themselves for entertainment (rather than simply being entertained, especially by TV) will have an easier time sitting and paying attention in school from the earliest grades.

For most students, the ability to succeed in school does not come easily. Young ones have to learn how to sit still, pay attention for lengthy periods of time to topics of conversation that may not be the most interesting, and get along with other students that may be distracting or difficult. The skills required for school success take time, focus and perseverance. Decreasing media exposure will assist your child with school success by increasing her attention span, forcing her to use her imagination, and decreasing distracting sexual and violent images in her brain. A simple rule about TV or movie watching or video game playing that make these activities out of bounds until homework or study time is finished will help. If your child comes home without homework, assign reading—even read the newspaper and talk about current events so that some time daily at home is set aside for learning.

Have your children spend some time outdoors, using their bodies to ride bikes, run, take a walk, shoot some baskets or throw a ball around. Our children's bodies are changing. This generation of children is the most overweight ever (even with the incredible contradiction of girls' starving themselves to death to fit our cultural role model for attractiveness) as a result of too much passive activity and not enough active use of their bodies. According to Dr. William Dietz of the New England Medical Center in Boston, the prevalence of obesity in children aged 12-17 increases by 2% for each hour of TV watched through the day. Too much TV and snacking, video game playing or movie watching is dangerous not only to our children's mental, emotional and educational health but to their physical health as well. The only influence that can truly affect this is the influence of home.

What can you do about all the cultural influence? Change the amount of time your family spends exposed to it. How will you know what to eliminate? Through the logs you have kept. Once the family has kept their logs of TV, movies and video game time, turn everything off. Go unplugged for one week. Don't watch a single TV show, rent a single movie, or play a single video game—NOTHING for one whole week. I'd like it to be three weeks, but I fear no one would actually go that long. The unplugging is hard, but it is also very important to resensitize you.

All of us have become desensitized by our culture. We can watch an episode of "Friends" and not be horrified by the promiscuity. We can listen to an Eminem song and care about his freedom of expression, or we can look at the covers of magazines and not see that the focus is completely on sex and body image. We are all living with the frog in the pot; the changes have happened so gradually that all of us are affected, even us parents. To really see what our culture looks like, we have to clear our minds of the ever present images of sex and violence so that we can really see. Once you have cleared your mind, watch again. Make decisions. Stick with them. Use your loving parental authority to establish limits and guidelines for your family entertainment.

Things to Think About

- Do you know what your children's favorite TV shows are? Have you ever watched with them?
- Do you have any rules about TV?
- Do your children have television in their rooms?
- Do you have rules about movies?
- Do you pay attention to ratings for TV, movies, music and video games? If not, why not?
- Have you ever played video games with your children? What is their favorite? Does it involve death and killing?
- What magazines come to your house by subscription? Do you take a look at your children's magazines?
- Have you ever read the lyrics from your children's CD's? Did you discuss what you thought of them with your child?
- Do your child's extracurricular activities interfere with family or church time? What can you do to change this? Talk to the coach or teacher? Could your child sit out of practices or lessons when they do interfere?

- Does your child have a hobby or interest? How can you encourage him to develop one?

Things to Do

- Pray about your children's exposure to popular culture. Ask God to reveal to you the areas in which you should pay closer attention.
- Have each family member keep a log of shows and movies watched and video games played for one week.
- Unplug all entertainment for everyone (including Mom and Dad) for at least one week, preferably three. Use the time to play games, talk, take walks, have conversation during dinner, and enjoy each other!
- Watch TV together. Set aside time to watch your child's favorite shows.
- Develop structure for TV time. Decide how much, at what hours and what type of content is acceptable.
- Develop structure for movie watching. Don't assume action movies are okay because it is "only action."
- Pay attention to ratings on movies, TV, video games and music. Use them to decide what is or is not appropriate.
- Play your child's favorite video games together. Is this how you want your child spending his or her time?
- Develop limits for video game playing. Amount of time and content should be parental decisions.
- Encourage a child who has lots of time for TV, games, and movies to develop a hobby, join a group or participate in an extracurricular activity. This is of utmost importance if your child is home alone for extended periods of time after school.
- Monitor the activities of a busy child. Choose parameters regarding time away from the family, interference with church, or health to determine which activities should continue and which should be limited.

Scripture to Remember

- 1 Thessalonians 5:15 - See that no one renders evil for evil to anyone, but always pursue what is good both for yourselves and for all.
- Philippians 2:15 - That you may become blameless and harmless, children of God without fault in the midst of a crooked and perverse generation, among whom you shine as lights in the world.
- James 1:27 (NIV) - Keep oneself from being polluted by the world.
- Romans 8:6-7 (NIV) - The mind of sinful man is death, but the mind controlled by the Spirit is life and peace; the sinful mind is hostile to God.
- Matthew 7:13 - Enter by the narrow gate; for wide is the gate and broad is the way that leads to destruction and there are many who go in by it.
- Matthew 16:23 - Get behind me, Satan! You are an offense to Me, for you are not mindful of the things of God, but the things of men.
- James 4:7-8 - Therefore submit to God. Resist the devil and he will flee from you. Draw near to God and He will draw near to you.
- Romans 12:2 - Do not be conformed to this world . . . that you may prove what is that good and acceptable and perfect will of God.
- 1 Timothy 4:12 - Let no one despise your youth, but be an example to the believers in word, in conduct, in love, in spirit, in faith, in purity.

Children do not develop the ability to think abstractly until well into adolescence. God is an abstract concept. We need to help our child understand who God is and why God matters. We can show them the way to God and His desires, that which is unseen, by showing them the way to fulfill parental desires, that which is seen. This is the most important job we have.

10

FAITH & Prayer

One snowy night a little boy and his dad were watching a movie and eating popcorn in front of a fire inside their nice warm house when the little boy heard banging against the window. He got up and looked out the window and saw small birds flying into the glass, trying to get into the warmth of the house. The little boy was compelled to go outside and try to save the little birds. So he and his dad went outside into the cold to try to help the birds. After trying one or two ideas, they had the thought of herding the birds into the garage where they could be warm and safe from the snow. They tried several different ways to encourage the little birds into the garage, but the birds were afraid and confused and couldn't be led to the safe place. In frustration the little boy said to his dad, "If only I could become a bird for a few minutes, then I could show them what to do so they could be safe."

Moses was eighty years old when God asked him to lead the Israelites out of Egypt back to the Promised Land. At first Moses protested, "I don't know how to do this, I wouldn't be very good at this, you should pick someone else." God said, "I will certainly be with you..." (Exodus 3:12).

How many of us have ever felt, "I don't know how to do this"? Have you ever had worries concerning your child you didn't know how to resolve? Have you ever not known what words to say in a tough situation with your child? Have you ever felt ill-equipped to do the job of raising him? You are not alone. Every person who has ever been called to do something for God has, at some time or another, not been sure it could be done—all the way back to Moses.

The advantage we have as Christians is that we can call on God, to invite Him to "help us" as we try to do His will in the raising of our children. Our child is a gift that we receive from God. His desire is that we demonstrate our gratitude for this gift by bringing this child to Him as she grows to adulthood. He tells us to "let the little children come to me, and do not hinder them, for the kingdom of heaven belongs to such as these" (Matthew 19:14, NIV). We bring our child to God through prayer. We pray with and for our children, both individually and as a family. Our goal is to establish the relationship that will not only provide strength, courage, and wisdom for this life but also will open the door for our children to establish their own saving relationship with Jesus Christ, bringing them to eternal life.

When I work with seventh graders, we use the Ten Commandments for guidance in moral decision-making. The Ten Commandments put parents in a very important place: the middle. Look at the first four commandments (paraphrased):

1. I am the Lord your God; have no other gods before me.
2. Do not worship idols.
3. Do not take the Lord's name in vain.
4. Keep the Sabbath Holy.

These all have to do with our relationship with God. Look at the last five commandments (paraphrased):

6. Do not kill.
7. Do not commit adultery.
8. Do not steal.

9. Do not lie.
10. Do not want what isn't yours.

These all have to do with our relationship with each other. The fifth commandment is, "Honor your mother and father, that your days may be long upon the land which the Lord has given you" (Exodus 20:12).

There are two things to note about this commandment: It is the only commandment with a promise (Ephesians 6:1-2), and it is right in the middle between our relationship with God and our relationship with others. The fact that God gives us a promise of long life when we honor our mother and father emphasizes to us just how important it is to Him that we do this. Trusting that God doesn't do anything by accident, I trust that we parents are in the middle for a reason. We have a job to do. We are the bridge between our child's relationship with others and their relationship with God.

Talk About Faith

Children do not develop the ability to think abstractly until well into adolescence. God is an abstract concept. We need to help our child understand who God is and why God matters. We can show them the way to God and His desires, that which is unseen, by showing them the way to fulfill parental desires, that which is seen. This is the most important job we have.

Consider the hours we spend worrying about our child's *earthly* life: potty training, pacifiers, preschool, kindergarten, homework, braces, sports, activities, high school, dating, college, marriage. (Even just the wedding!) Some of these assume a huge portion of our time and energy as our child grows.

Now consider the hours we spend preparing our child for *eternal* life. How does that match up? One hour a week at church? Evening prayers when the children are small? Grace at the dinner table? Does your child's eternal life ever assume a part of the time and energy of your day? Is helping your child connect with God a part of your family life? It should be!

Study after study demonstrates the effect faith has on children and teenagers. One hour per week in church is one of the forty assets the Search Institute identifies as helping children with resiliency (see Appendix C in the leader's guide to the video series to *Sex as God's Gift*, page 48). We have learned that the connection to faith helps to decrease high risk behaviors and gives children a sense of security and tradition. Practice of faith provides children with an opportunity to belong to a community of value.

Talking about faith provides the opportunity for endless conversation. An ongoing conversation we have had for years in our family was about Noah, the flood and the dinosaurs, and how they all fit into history. A young friend of ours would start the conversation every time we had a long car ride. We had some pretty interesting conjectures and theories. We never came up with an answer, but we talked about God, history, theology and different beliefs for many hours over several years. These conversations helped to shape our children's faith and broaden their thinking about God and His care for us. It has been a great debate.

Show Them Faith

The Commandments show us that we must have concern for our child's eternal life. We have to teach him to obey, and he learns how to obey God by obeying us. We teach our child to show respect to God by his showing respect to us. We teach our child how to speak to God and about God by expecting him to speak correctly to us, by not accepting the use of God's name in a casual or irreverent way. We have the responsibility to role-model obedience, respect, kindness, compassion and faith for our child. We have the responsibility to model God's expectations of us through our expectations of our child. We fail our child if we don't put him on the path of eternal life. No matter how much we do for him to satisfy his earthly needs, we have failed if we don't show him the way to eternal life in paradise with God.

We live in a culture that talks about "spirituality" without having anything to do with God. Our children are bombarded with messages about doing what they want to do, not doing what God wants them to do. Our culture rationalizes all kinds of ungodly behaviors, from cheating on your wife to calling abortion a "choice." We live at a time when it is acceptable to be anything but Christian. In this environment, Christians must be diligent. We are the remnant who must pass our faith on to the next generation. If our children do not have the opportunity to recognize faith and develop their own faith in God within the family, they may not have exposure to the saving grace of Christ anywhere else.

The teenagers I see always want to know how God can deny anyone access to heaven just because they didn't believe in Him on earth. I reply with a question: "Why would you *want* to spend eternity with God if you thought He didn't exist?" God gave us all the gift of free will. God loves us perfectly. He loves us enough not to control our every thought or action. He loves us enough to let us decide whether or not we will love Him back. If you believe we will go somewhere after this life, I hope that you also believe that we have a choice about where we go. Where we spend eternity is not a random choice made by a disinterested God. God's preference, frequently stated throughout Scripture, is that we spend eternity in peace and joy with Him. He has prepared a place for each of us, including you and your child. God's preparation for your child's eternal life has long been completed. Now the rest is up to you and your child. You show your child the way, but your child makes the decision about the relationship. If you believe there is a heaven and a hell, would you not want to provide your child with an introduction to the relationship that is necessary for heaven? That relationship is with Jesus Christ.

Christ came to the world to show us the way. Most importantly, He showed us the way to His Father, but He also showed us the way to treat one another while we are here. He showed us how to be loving and righteous and how to have appropriate expectations, how to be parents, and how to teach. But most important, He showed us what we need—Him! He showed us the way to the Father. Our responsibility is to show our children the way in the same manner Jesus showed us. He came to earth as a human to show us the way, to decrease our confusion and to clarify our direction. He did that for us to make our paths straight.

Consider Christ's approach to us: He leads us along gently but firmly. He knows exactly where He wants us. He meets us wherever we are and brings us to where He wants us to be with kindness and understanding of our challenges. Debate or discussion on our part is fruitless: God knows what is best for us. If we choose to live our lives without Him, we will experience the consequences. If we choose to include Him in our lives, we will experience the benefits. It is that simple and complicated at the same time. God is faithful—always. If we parents could use just some of God's ways with our children, how much more joyful and peace-filled our lives would be.

This is where prayer comes in. We are not God; we are human. We are not perfect; we will make mistakes; we will feel weak; we will lack courage; we will be confused and unsure. Often we are not sure what we should do, how we should handle our children, or how to respond to some of the challenges of childrearing. Sometimes it is difficult to be kind instead of harsh and compassionate instead of angry, or to show our child the way instead of giving up. There is one thing we can do that really works. WE MUST PRAY!!

We follow Jesus' example of faith and dependency when we pray. We make our best choices when we open our lives to God's desires for us and ask Him to use us as vessels for His will to be done (the prayer that never fails: "Your will be done.") We can't do this without prayer.

Prayer is our communication with God. If you think of the people you are closest to, you will probably realize that you communicate with them frequently. How close would you be with someone you talked to only when you had trouble? How good would your friend be if she only contacted you when she needed or wanted something? How about if the trouble she was in time after time was of her own doing but she wanted you to undo it? How would you feel if you constantly gave your friend advice, a break, sympathy and love but she continued to go out and do the same behaviors over and over again? Scripture tells us God's mind is not our mind, and His ways are not our ways. But we can try to imagine His response to us if we are uninterested, unfaithful and ungracious receivers of His many gifts.

If we knew there was someone we could talk to about our child every day who would listen carefully and compassionately, who could change our child's life for the better, and who could offer our child a promise of love, goodness, kindness, patience, self-control, peace, joy and faithfulness (the fruits of the spirit in Galatians 5:22), would we talk to him? If we knew there was someone who would be with our child ALL THE TIME to protect her from harm, to show her the right response, and to comfort her in times of trouble, would we talk to Him? If we knew our child had a chance to live forever in peace and harmony, without tears or sadness, death or pain and all it took was a daily conversation, would we have it?

For me the answer could only be YES!! There is someone who offers our child eternal life. There is someone who will listen to us compassionately and carefully, who can be with our child all the time, and who can wipe away death, sorrow and pain for our child. That someone is Jesus Christ. He promises us no one comes to the Father except through the Son. He promises us He will save us from our own sins. He promises us, "Certainly, I will be with you." What we have to do to connect to those promises is pray.

175

Prayer will change the life of your family your child particularly both now and for eternity. It would be easy to be afraid to invite these changes into your life, but I promise you that these are changes for the better. God's way is always better than ours.

How Should We Worship & Pray?

In Community

We worship and pray communally in church. This is the way we stay in touch with other believers. We come together to strengthen one another's faith, to support each other and to become the "Body of Christ," each of us having a role. Our children learn how to worship and pray in community by being a part. So our first responsibility to our children's eternal life is to see that they participate in a community of faith. This means that you go with your child to church, become engaged in the community of faith, and participate in any way you can, big or small. You belong.

At our church, you can participate by seating people before service or passing the collection basket. You can sit on the finance board, clean the church, teach religious education or join a weekly prayer group. You can sing in the choir or you can sing in your seat, being friendly and welcoming to the person next to you. Most communities of faith have many jobs that are required for the running of the church. What job can you and your family participate in? Don't be shy. Speak up. Churches desire the involvement of their members.

I go to many churches every year, and they all are constantly thinking of ways to get the members involved. It is a challenge that faces communities of faith everywhere. Everyone loves a cheerful giver, particularly if you can give a little of your time. Offer an hour a week or an hour a month. If your church doesn't have a job for you, create one. Are there people in your congregation who need help with their homes? Can you and your child spend a Saturday afternoon raking someone's leaves? Can you shop for a family that may be struggling to afford food (just one bag of groceries a week)? Can you visit a shut-in? All of these acts will bond you to your faith community. Bring your child along. You may meet some resistance at first, but once you develop the habit, it will be something you both look forward to.

Your child's participation in a peer Bible study or activity group cannot be overemphasized. Of course, within the boundaries discussed before (not overdoing it with activities outside the home), her involvement can prove to be valuable in providing positive peer pressure and active fellowship for your teen. In such groups, the Christian faith and values of your family usually are reinforced in your church's youth group. This also would give your family the opportunity to get to know other families and teens that face the same challenges with popular culture and daily living. However, do not get your child involved in these activities with blind trust. Get to know the youth leader and his family, if possible. He should share with you his goals for the youth group as well as work with you in helping your child develop faith in God and a desire to serve Him.

Do not forget that gathering as a community to pray together could be a tremendous blessing to your church leaders as well as to each other. Remember that God is listening where two or three are gathered together in his name in prayer (Matthew 18:20). Community prayer is a wonderful way for you and your child to understand your parts within the Body of Christ in His service.

As a Family

The second way to connect is through family prayer. Pray together as a family at the dinner table. Grace before meals is a great way to start to pray with each other. It's nice to hold hands around the table and thank God for all your blessings. A traditional prayer is a fine way to begin, but it is very nice to personalize your prayer:

Bless us, oh Lord, for these Thy gifts which we are about to receive from Your bounty through Christ our Lord. Amen.

Thank you, God, for this day. We pray for our neighbor who is having treatment for cancer. Please touch her with your healing hand, and provide her family with the strength they need to help her through this.

We pray for James in school whose parents are getting divorced. We thank you that Dad's meeting went well. Please help Susan study hard for her math test tonight. Amen.

In our house, when we have a lot of people that we are praying for, we keep a list to be sure that we remember everyone. We cross people off as their specific requests are answered. When we pray together as a family we have the opportunity to see how God answers prayers. We learn that He answers prayers in His own time and His own way and that, in the long run, God's way is the right way even when we hoped His way would be different.

Pray when you get in the car for a long trip; pray a prayer of gratitude when you arrive home safely. Pray in the morning together before you start your day; pray in times of need and in times of gratitude. Touch one another when you pray together; join together as a family physically and spiritually.

Don't be shy about praying as a family in front of others. When your children's friends eat with you, invite them into your prayer. Reach out to hold the hand of your child's friend. We have found our visiting friends to be very open to this experience, even those who don't pray at home. You'll never guess how far your family prayer will go. Inviting others into your family prayers will plant seeds of faith that may flower many years down the road.

Individually with Each Child

Set aside time each day to pray with your children individually. The younger they are when you begin, the easier it is to continue praying together one on one as they get older. Pray together at bedtime. Thank God for your day; thank Him for the blessings in your life. In our house, Maggie and I pray together each night before she goes to sleep. It is a comforting part of our nighttime ritual. Once Maggie is tucked in, nice and cozy, we calm our minds, take a deep breath, and say "Let's pray."

We always thank God first for many of the things that make our lives so nice; we thank God that "our boys" (my husband and son) make us laugh. We thank God for our pets, for the weather of the day, for our extended family; and we ask Him to watch over anyone who is traveling, unhappy or unhealthy. We thank God for our school, for the love we have in our lives, and for our health. We ask God to take good care of Maggie's future husband. We pray for those who are sick or suffering because of family unhappiness or money trouble. We try to pray for as many people by name as we can, and we try to vary our prayers from night to night. We ask God to give us servant's hearts and to let us show someone we belong to God through our words or actions the next day.

Our prayers take a shorter time to say than you just spent reading them, but they are one of the most important times of the day. When we pray together, we invite God into our daily family lives. He, more than anyone, can influence how we treat each other as a family, what our values and goals are, and how much joy we experience in daily living. Praying together shows our teens how to talk to God, how to demonstrate gratitude, and how to intercede for someone smaller, weaker or less fortunate than you. Praying together opens the door for your child to begin to develop his own personal, prayerful relationship with their Lord.

By praying together, we are teaching our children how to pray alone. The temptation in prayer is to be superficial, to go over the surface issues, instead of looking deep into your heart to discover what you are grateful for, where you are needy, who is needy around you. We have a great example of how to pray from the prophet Nehemiah in the Old Testament (1:5):

> I pray, Lord God of Heaven, O Great and awesome God, You who keep Your covenant and mercy with those who love You and keep Your commandments, Please let Your ear be attentive and Your eyes open that You may hear the prayer of Your servant which I pray before You now, day and night.

I like this passage as an example of how to approach God in our daily prayer. Be reverent, be respectful, be grateful, and ask God to hear your prayer. Pray frequently. When I assign middle and high school students the homework of praying for themselves every day, I tell them to begin the practice of praying while they are brushing their teeth. Even though this is not as reverent as we would like, it will at least begin the habit.

Every night when they brush their teeth, I tell them, they should review their day with God in their mind:

> Hello, God. It's me. Today was a pretty good day; these are the good parts of my day (tell Him the highlights); these are the tough parts of my day (tell Him your struggles). These are the people I am worried about; these are the people I am grateful for. Be with me tomorrow to show me the way you want me to be. Amen.

Every morning when they brush their teeth, they should go over the upcoming day in their minds with God.

> Good morning, God. Thank you for being with me through the night. Please be with me today as I . . . (tell

Him what you are facing today). Help me be a good (friend, brother, sister, student). Watch over me as I (take this test, talk to my friends, meet with the coach, try out for this sport). Help me to do your will today. Amen.

At first, I tell the children just to pray that they remember to pray. As the praying becomes easier, as the habit develops, spend more time in prayer. Set aside time to pray when you are not brushing your teeth. Begin to use Scripture to pray during your quiet time. One mom reported to me that her eighth grade son got in the car after one of my programs and excitedly said, "Mom, did you know that when you talk to God, that is praying?" He was incredulous, thinking that praying had to be formal, that using words written by someone else was the way to connect with God rather than using words that come from your heart.

If you are the parent of a middle school or high school student, you could start them praying by praying first as a family, then individually with your child, then reminding them to pray on their own when you remind them to brush their teeth. If your child is younger, start off praying as a family, move to praying as an individual, and then you will be able to move to simply reminding your child to pray at bedtime, skipping the praying during the teeth-brushing phase.

Like discipline, the younger you begin praying with your child, the easier it is to establish as a habit. Once the habit is established, it is up to you, the parents, to keep it going during the middle and high school years. By the junior year in high school, many of the good habits we work hard to establish during the first 16 or 17 years of life begin to take hold if we sustain the habit. These habits, like praying, begin to belong to your teenager—begin to become their own personal habit, no longer just family habits—after practicing them under parental guidance for many years. We are tempted to decrease our vigilance and reminders during middle school. It may feel awkward to tell your thirteen year old to brush his teeth and pray, but don't give up! Your child continues to need your reminders and expectations until the habit belongs to her. You may want to change how your reminders sound. We prefer the humorous approach in our house, a little gentle teasing that has a reminder wrapped up in a little laugh.

We remind our children to brush their teeth more than 9,000 times before they remember to brush their teeth consistently on their own. Tooth brushing is the most basic form of personal hygiene that takes 90 seconds twice a day. In order for our children to remember to do this, we have to remind them daily for many years. We need to realize that this type of frequency is necessary for any life-long pattern to be established, especially if it is something more complicated than teeth brushing.

For Our Children

The third way to connect is intercessory prayer. Parents' prayers are powerful before the Lord. We can discuss our innermost concerns about our child with the Lord, and He can actually make a difference.

I recommend setting aside special time each day to bring your children to God in prayer. Get on your knees. Bring your children by name to God. Share with Him your worries about your child, and thank Him for your children's strengths. Include Him in your children's day-to-day life. Let your children know you are praying. We even pray for our children when they have tests: they tell us what time the test is, and I pray that they will remember everything they studied.

Begin your day with prayer for your children. Recall each child by name. Think of each child's day, and let God know where you think the challenges will be. Thank God for the strengths your child may demonstrate throughout the day. Open your heart and let God see in. Even when you can't imagine how to begin to pray, God promises His Spirit to help us: "For we do not know what we should pray for as we ought, but the Spirit Himself makes intercession for us with groaning, which cannot be uttered" (Romans 8:26).

End each day with prayer for your children. Do you have little ones that don't sleep through the night? Ask for a good night's sleep. Do you have a middle school daughter who doesn't tell you what is in her heart or life? Pray for God to open a door for conversation together. Do you have a child who is lonely? Pray for a friend. Do you have a child who loves risk? Pray for his safety. Do you need patience with an issue with your child? Ask for it. Do you need a different style of interacting with your child? Have the Lord show you the way. Remember God promises us, "Whatever you ask for in prayer, *believing*, you shall receive" (Matthew 21:22, italics mine).

I get consistent positive feedback from parents who start to pray in earnest for their children. Parents who turn to God for their child's specific needs often will find these needs being met in ways they never anticipated. God does not always answer our prayers in our timing or in our way, but when we ask believing, we will find an answer.

Let's go back to Moses. He had a job he didn't think he was capable of. He was doing this huge job on faith alone, which was shaky at times. He was responsible for hundreds of Israelites, their wives and children, their livestock and all their earthly possessions. The Israelites were unhappy, complaining, and rebellious; they were forgetful of all the miracles God performed for them (the parting of the Red Sea, manna from heaven, the saving of all their firstborns at Passover). Moses was eighty years old and was spending forty years in the desert just trying to get the Israelites to the place God had promised, when he rather would have been doing something else.

How did Moses handle this overwhelming responsibility? He prayed and interceded, face down on the ground before the Lord, on behalf of his charges. It wasn't easy. It took much longer than he thought. He didn't always feel up to the task. His charges were rebellious, dissatisfied and disobedient, so he prayed. And God certainly was with him.

How do we handle our overwhelming responsibility? We pray and intercede, on our knees in a quiet place, before the Lord, on behalf of our charges. We don't have an easy job. It is harder than we thought. It takes a long time to raise a child to adulthood, and we don't always feel up to the task. Our charges can be rebellious, disobedient and dissatisfied. So we pray. And God certainly will be with us.

Some Practical Considerations

Make an appointment with yourself to pray, clear your calendar, and pencil the time in. This is your session with God about your child. Keep this appointment as you would any other that you consider important. Find a quiet place where you are unlikely to be disturbed to pray. Turn on the answering machine, close your door, and just be quiet for a few moments before you begin.

Don't pray when you are so tired that you may fall asleep when praying. Although it is a nice practice to pray yourself to sleep at night, *this* prayer session requires wakefulness and attention.

Prayer takes practice. It may feel awkward at first to be talking to God without the structure of formal prayer. Keep trying. Ask God to help you find the words and the proper approach; ask Him to help you remember to pray.

If your mind wanders, ask God to refocus you. Ask Him to clear your mind and heart for prayer.

Scripture can help you to find the words to pray when it is difficult to come up with your own. Many people enjoy using a Daily Devotional Bible to begin their prayer time. Scripture can focus your thoughts towards prayer and towards issues you may want to cover with God such as patience, steadfastness, faithfulness, honor. (See Appendix I in the leader's guide to the video series *Sex as God's Gift* curriculum, page 55, for tips on choosing a Bible and how to use it.) Have a prayer partner, another mother or father to pray with and for. You can strengthen each other through prayer and fellowship. We started a prayer group for moms at our school which meets weekly to share concerns and pray aloud together. It is a great way to start the week. (See Appendix B, parent to parent, on page 220, for information on starting your own prayer group.) Participate in a Bible study. Get to know God through Scripture and through other men and women of faith. Many churches have regular study periods. Neighborhood studies are also popular. I once saw a bumper sticker that said, "Give your worries to God. He is up all night anyway." Good advice!

Things to Think About

- How much time and energy have you devoted to your child's eternal life?
- Have you introduced your child to God and provided an opportunity for your child to get to know Him?
- What are your prayer habits? Individually? As a family?
- Do you participate in community worship? If not, is it possible for you to do this?
- Which aspect of Christ do you model for your child?
- Which aspect of Christ would you like to begin or improve modeling now?

Things to Do

- Pray at the dinner table. Begin with a simple grace, then you can add your personal prayers before you eat each night.
- Pray at bedtime with each of your children if possible.
- Pray for each of your children each day.
- Pray for yourself and the job you have as a parent. Ask for the strength you need, and give thanks for the blessings of your children.

- Buy a Bible, preferably a daily devotional. Read it.
- Attend church together.
- Become a part of your church community. Which part of the body of Christ can you be?
- Provide opportunities to have conversations about God. This is more difficult with older children, but it can occur with perseverance.
- Find someone to pray with. Pray for others together.
- Remember to say "thank you" in your prayers.
- Join a Bible study.
- Encourage your child to join a Christian peer group.

Scripture to Remember

- James 5:16 - The effective, fervent prayer of the righteous avails much.
- Mark 11:24 - Therefore I say to you, whatever things you ask when you pray, believe that you receive them, and you will have them.
- Matthew 21:22 - And all things, whatever you ask in prayer believing, you will receive.
- Philippians 4:5-7 - Let your gentleness be known to all men. The Lord is at hand. Be anxious for nothing, but in everything by prayer and supplication, with thanksgiving let your requests be made known to God. And the peace of God, which surpasses all understanding, will guard your hearts and minds through Christ Jesus.
- Luke 1:37 - For with God nothing will be impossible.
- 1 Thessalonians 5:16-18 - Rejoice always. Pray without ceasing. In everything give thanks.
- Galatians 5:22 - But the fruit of the spirit is love, joy, peace, longsuffering, kindness, goodness, faithfulness, gentleness and self-control.
- Romans 8:26 - For we do not know what we should pray for as we ought, but the Spirit Himself makes intercession for us with groanings which can not be uttered.

- Proverbs 16:3 - Commit your works to the Lord, and your thoughts will be established.
- John 15:7 - If you abide in me and my words abide in you, you will ask what you desire, and it shall be granted to you.

To be independent requires self-discipline, planning, self-control and perseverance. Are you going to leave a legacy of discipline, love and support that will build the character traits necessary? We can't start to pay attention tomorrow. Now is the time; they are growing up right before your eyes. Now is the chance you have to raise up these children in the way they should go.

11

BEING the Parent

I had an attractive freshman girl come in to see me. She was afraid she had a sexually transmitted disease and wanted to know what to do. When I asked her how she got the disease, she told me she was on vacation with her mother in Mexico. Her mother and she went out to a local club. Her mother left early with a man and allowed her fifteen-year-old daughter to stay. She was in a foreign country, did not speak the language, and was underage in a local bar, abandoned by her mother. You can be sure this girl did not feel loved. So when an "old guy" asked her if she needed a ride, she said "yes." He did take her back to her hotel, eventually, after forcing her to participate in a variety of sex acts with him. She felt lucky to be alive. She never told her mother.

The law was not on this girl's side. She was able to go for testing and treatment of her sexually transmitted disease (yes, she had one!) without informing her mother. There was no safety net to catch the neglect this young girl experienced. While I can't imagine what this mother must have been thinking to leave her daughter in such peril, I do believe she needed to know the results of her abandonment.

The bottom line: We are responsible for the well-being of our children physically, emotionally and spiritually. No one else can do that job for us. We entrust our children to others all day—teachers, coaches, leaders and friends' parents throughout every week of their lives. But raising our child is not their job. Their job is to show our child what we can't, to teach our child what we may not know, and to broaden our child's perspective. But we have to raise our child. We are ultimately responsible.

Day to day most families experience some challenges to their family life. Few families escape without some kind of obstacle to overcome. It is not easy being the grown-up. It is not easy being ultimately responsible for the well-being of another human being. It is not easy being a loving, firm, compassionate, God-fearing role model for someone who is in the process of becoming. The task becomes even more challenging when we work outside of our homes, keep our families fed, clothed and schooled and meet their ever changing needs. No wonder parents are tired! Whew!

Nevertheless, we have to be the parent. We have to fulfill our responsibility to our child, our community, our extended family, ourselves and, most importantly, our God. I asked you in an earlier chapter to think about the gift God gave you when He gave you this child. Think about holding this baby in your arms for the first time. Think about the miracle of this child's birth. The gift of life is precious indeed.

Is this child your first, middle or last? What did you learn about yourself as a result of this child's entering your life? What have you learned most recently from this child? It is almost impossible for us to imagine life without this child, so what do we do to be grateful? We "raise up our child in the way he should go so that when he is old he won't depart from it" (Proverbs 22:6).

We are told, "Let us not become weary in doing good, for you will reap a harvest at the proper time if you do not give up" (Galatians 6:9). I think this passage is especially for parents of today. It would be so easy to become weary of doing good. We could stop fighting the popular culture, throw up our arms and say, "My children are going to see (hear, learn, know about, do) this anyway, so why bother?" This thinking gives us permission to stop doing our job, to step back from our parental responsibilities and allow our children to grow up without the limits, structure and guidance that are necessary to be a self-respecting, contributing adult.

As hard as this is for many parents to believe, our children prefer the limits. Most of the late middle school and early high school students I see who have parents that provide close boundaries do not mind the boundaries. The girls and boys I see who have chosen to wait for sexual intimacy have parents who provide loving boundaries. The key to success with limits is that they are applied with a heavy dose of love. The combination of the two protects children and helps them be better decision makers.

We are warned not to become weary. Even though we will feel weary and want to give up, we must not give in. We must press on for the sake of the children. They are the most valuable thing we will leave behind. Parents, with the long view, must leave a legacy not just for this life but for eternal life as well. Our job is first to introduce our child to a saving relationship with Jesus Christ, and second to help them become independent, to leave us and live productive lives of their own.

To be independent requires self-discipline, planning, self-control and perseverance. Are you going to leave a legacy of discipline, love and support that will build the character traits necessary? You can't start to pay attention tomorrow. Now is the time; they are growing up right before your eyes. Now is the chance you have to raise up these children in the way they should go.

What is a busy parent to do? Look at the three "L's."

LOVE Them So They Can Feel It

This is first. Love them. Each of us has a need and desire to be loved. The way we love our children is the pathway to their adult security and relationship development. We want to love them so they can feel it.

By middle school many children become horrified by public displays of affection from their parents. They no longer want us to touch them in public, show verbal affection, or, sometimes even act like we know them. Don't take this to mean they don't want us to tell them we love them anymore, just not in front of their friends. Don't take this to mean they don't want us to hug or kiss them anymore, just not outside of the house. Even if they shrug their shoulders and hang their arms limply at their sides when you hug them at home, make reassuring physical contact. Discomfort with parental affection can begin as early as fourth or fifth grade, but will lessen as your child matures. If you stop showing physical affection during this time, it may be difficult to reestablish contact.

Parents have approached me after several recent seminars in attempts to dissuade me from encouraging physical affection between parent and child because of the risk of sexual molestation. While inappropriate contact does occur in unhealthy families, a parent with a healthy view of relationships has the ability to show their child what love is. Both our daughters and our sons need to know that loving someone should not be painful, nor should it be about one person's expectations of another or what you will do for someone else. Parents have the opportunity to demonstrate this for their child through demonstrations of physical affection such as hugging and kissing from parent to child. Parents also have the opportunity to demonstrate healthy love through the role-modeling in their own relationships. Our children learn far more from watching us than we can imagine.

It is imperative that our daughters feel loved by their families. She needs to be valued at home to value herself. It is all too easy for a teenage daughter to go looking for love in all the wrong places if she does not feel loved at home. Fathers provide an important key to the way a daughter believes women should be loved. A father who demonstrates affection by hugging his daughter, hugging his wife in the kitchen (and gets "caught" by the children), and treats his family with gentleness, humor and respect, will help his daughters and sons see the way a man should be. Our children should know we love them NO MATTER WHAT.

I was working in a suburban private high school with ninth- through twelfth-grade students. On the last day we have private sessions for any student who wants to have fifteen minutes on his own with me to discuss any problems or ask any questions. The story at the beginning of the chapter describes one of these sessions. What a tragic situation for this girl! No one to protect her, no one to show her that love doesn't have to be painful, no one to show her the way to peace and happiness. (Her mom clearly has no idea how to get there.) She is destined for one unsatisfactory sexual encounter after another, being used by men for their own pleasure, never knowing that there is another way. This is a dramatic example of what happens to teen girls when they are not well-loved.

Just telling our children we love them is not enough. It is necessary but not complete. They learn that we love them from our words. They understand we love them from our actions. Children who feel protected feel loved. Parents who say, "I love you too much to let you do that," do their children a big favor. Parents who are able to say, "No, that is not good for you," have children who feel loved. Parents who monitor their children have children who feel protected, and parents who supervise their children have children who feel cared for. Parents who take time to talk with and listen to their children have children who feel valued.

We falsely imagine that our children will feel loved if we never deny them anything. We think that saying "no" to our children will make them feel deprived, underprivileged, unloved. The opposite is true. The more our children feel protected (even from themselves), the more they feel loved. It seems to me from the parents I meet that we are afraid of loving our children in this way. We fear they will misinterpret our love and leave us, go to the big city and become drug-addicted prostitutes just because we say "no." I know that sounds dramatic, but that is what parents are afraid of—rebellion. Parents want their children to like them more than respect them. How can a child respect a parent who can't say "no" to him?

One day I was doing a radio show with a gentleman who is involved in bringing character education to the schools. He told me that he had just brought a friend of his to the airport to go back to England after a short visit. As they were driving to the airport, the friend said that the parents in America made an impression on him: they were afraid of their children; the fear was on the wrong side of the equation.

I agree. No, I don't think our children should be afraid of us because we will harm them in any way. I don't think we should have discipline without love because that is punitive and ineffective, but we also should not have love without discipline. But I do think our children should not want to let us down. They should fear disappointing us. They should fear how we will respond if they don't live up to our standards of behavior. When I ask the children what they would prefer, a mad parent or a disappointed parent, the universal response is mad. We get over it. We don't usually stick to our punishments. Mad goes away. Disappointment lasts. It happens when a trust is broken. It changes our view of our child. They do not like this. Disappointment makes more of an impact than just "getting mad."

I was very well loved growing up. I had a happy, stable home life with parents who showed each other and us five children plenty of affection. That was very nice. Within all the love and affection, my mother ruled with an iron hand. My father was very good at "drawing the line." My parents were tough. We couldn't get away with anything. They knew all the tricks we were up to, and they stopped us. My mother was an excellent example of how to apply guilt effectively. She would say "It would break my heart if you. . . ." It worked like a charm. Sure, we had our scrapes and got into some trouble. We did some things we weren't supposed to do. But small infractions felt like big ones, and there are some things I would never do for fear of disappointing my mother. I knew she wasn't going to flip out, beat me, disown me or even scream at me. But I knew my actions could "break her heart," and that was something she took a long time to recover from. I would go out of my way to avoid breaking my mother's heart. That choice kept me from making many bad decisions during high school. I'm grateful for her strictness to this day. Her loving toughness with me showed me how to have loving toughness for my children.

Today, I meet very few parents who feel comfortable "drawing the line" as my parents did. Our belief that "they are going to do it anyway" stops parents from having clearly defined expectations for their children's behavior. With no clear rules, our children think everything is okay, so they push further and further into high-risk activities. All you have to do is read *Ophelia Speaks* to see the results of our no-limits child rearing. Our children need for us to love them so they can "feel" it.

Provide LIMITS

Developmentally, adolescence is the time our children move from concrete to abstract thinking. They are working toward becoming abstract thinkers, but they are not completely there yet. Like our two year old, our fifteen year old is yearning for independence and has great desire to do things on her own; but she does not yet have the skill or maturity to do it. Physical readiness follows emotional desire. This is especially true in today's culture. Our eighteen month old wants to go up and down the stairs alone, our two year old wants to climb the bookcases, our four year old wants to cross the street without us, our fifteen year old wants to be sexually active. The same developmental activity is happening. We would no more let our four year old cross the street alone than we would leave him outside by himself all night. We need to develop that same protectiveness towards our teen.

Our teens need to bump up against boundaries to know where they are. If we move the boundary every time they push against it, they will never understand the boundaries. We have to show them. They are not being "bad" when they complain and ask why. They are not out of line when they question our decision. They are looking for the boundaries. They depend upon us to show them the limits. If we don't show them someone else will have to. That someone else may be at school or the community in which the consequences are much greater. If we intervene with school or community consequences, we hinder our child from learning the limits necessary to be productive in society.

Think about your adult life. Do you get everything you want? Are you able to do everything you want to? In his book John Rosemond's *Six Point Plan for Raising Happy, Healthy Children*, the author suggests making a list of everything you want. Let your fantasy run wild, and list your unrealistic desires as well as the wishes you might receive. Then go back over the list and put a check mark next to the items you will actually get in the next five years. Mr. Rosemond's work has shown him that most adults can realistically expect to have 15-20% of what they want in five years.[4] Now, do the same for your child. When you check items off your child's list, remember to include gifts from grandparents, other relatives and friends. How much will your child have in the next twelve months? If you learn to live with 15% of what you want, how will your child learn to live with that if he is accustomed to 75%, the average amount a child can expect in the next twelve months?

His solution is to give our children more Vitamin N:

This vital nutrient consists simply of the most character-building two letter word in the English language.
Vitamin N is as important to a child's healthy growth

and development as Vitamins A, B, and C. Unfortunately, many, if not most, of today's children suffer from Vitamin N deficiency. They have been overindulged by well-meaning parents who've given them far too much of what they want and far too little of what they truly need.[5]

Do you know what he is talking about? The word "NO."

If we focus on the long term, we can see the benefits of a little frustration. The way we learn to wait is by waiting. The way we learn to keep working forward even if things aren't going our way is by going forward; the way we learn to persevere is by persevering. There is no other way to develop the skills needed for character than by practicing them. In the same way our child will not learn to play the piano or multiply or shoot baskets from the foul line without practice. They will not learn the more important lessons of character without practicing also. It is up to us to provide the opportunities.

We provide many of these opportunities when we impose limits on our child. We don't impose limits just for the sake of frustrating our child, although that may happen (and is good for them). We impose limits to show our child the difference between "want" and "need." We impose limits to help our child avoid unhealthy, risky situations, to manage the input of popular culture into our child's life, and to prepare our child for adulthood.

When we expect our child to wait for something, we give our child practice in waiting for what he wants. When we expect our child to obey us, we give her practice in respecting authority. When we have boundaries in our lives that are different from others, we teach our child that doing what is right isn't always doing what is popular. The simple rule about respecting the rating system (e.g., no R-rated movies until you are at least seventeen, if at all; no M-rated video games until you are mature) provides our child with all of those opportunities to practice.

197

It is challenging to begin to impose limits when your child is a teenager if you have never had limits in your household before. Expect unhappiness. None of us enjoy limits. But we all need them. Our culture reinforces a "no limits" mentality. Limits provide safety to a growing, changing adolescent. There is security in knowing just how far you can go. It is easier to make decisions if you know what is expected.

Limits are not punitive; they are protective as a source of opportunity for maturing. It is our job to help our children get ready for independence. That means they need practice at waiting for what they want, respecting authority, and standing up for what is right, even when it is difficult. If we keep this in mind as we establish boundaries and talk to our children about them, it will be easier for us to avoid having an argument. We need to trust that we are doing what is best for our child when we provide structure and discipline to his daily life. We need to keep our child's whole life in our mind, not just his teenage life. If we don't focus on the long-term benefits for our child, it is difficult for us to make the choices that are necessary to develop character. Our children depend upon us to have the long view for them as they are only capable of seeing the here and now. The long view comes with maturity. The parents are the mature ones in the relationship.

I want to caution you about being drawn into arguments about your limits. Your teen will probably have many valid points about why you should change your mind about a boundary. There may be times (although rare) when you should listen to your child and change your mind. Consider these suggestions:

- *Never change your mind because your child is having a tantrum.*

"I hate you. I hate you. You are the only parents who say no." "Why can't I go? Please, let me. I promise you just this

198

one time." When a tantrum happens, your child is giving you a very clear signal that she is not yet ready for independence. You want your child to show you that she can have strong feelings about something and not act on them before you allow more independence. Tantrums demonstrate that this child must act on her feelings. Therefore, they are a signal for you to wait before you loosen the reins a little.

- *Never change your mind because your child gives you a time limit.*

"I have to know NOW, or I won't be able to go." We should never buy anything under pressure, including our child's desperate, immediate need to do something that came up only two minutes ago, and this offer will only last until NOW!!! Always say "no" unless there is compelling adult information that a "yes" is reasonable.

- *Never change your mind if you need more information, and your child is resistant to your getting it.*

If your child doesn't want you to talk with another parent about an activity, that is a warning sign that all may not be what you are being led to believe. Always reserve the right to talk to the parents with whom your child will be spending time. It is your responsibility to know who your child is with, who is in charge and what they will be doing.

- *Change your mind if you made your decision hastily without any information, and your child gives you information that eliminates your concerns.*

This would include having information from and about the adults that will be responsible for your child. This information should be presented to you in a calm and rational way.

Here are some areas in which boundaries are helpful for family life.

Behaviors

What do you expect of your children's behavior? Is yelling okay? Do you have rules about what type of language is considered acceptable? How about physical contact with each other (hitting, pinching)? How should your children disagree with you? With each other? How do you treat one another in the family? How do you expect your children to treat the other relatives? How about their friends? Yours? Do you have manners expectations at meal time?

Social life

Do you have a curfew, or do you discuss what time to be home after each event? Do you call houses where parties are going to be held? Do you have rules for dating? Does your child know your expectations regarding drinking, drug use and sexual activity? How about drinking and driving? Do you have a "rescue" plan if your teen gets into a situation in which he feels over his head? ("Call us at any time, and we will come get you.") Do you have rules for parties at your house? Do you expect to know your children's friends?

Popular culture

Do you have guidelines regarding movies, TV and video games? Do your children know how you feel about some of the messages of popular entertainment? Are you familiar with your children's choices of entertainment? Are you comfortable with them?

School

Does your child know your expectations about school? Do you work cooperatively with your child's school about discipline and limits? Do you support any disciplinary action your child's school or teachers must make for your child? Does your child have a designated time for homework or quiet reading if homework isn't assigned? Do you know your child's grades before the report card comes home, or are the grades a surprise? Do you participate in school activities? Do you go to parents' nights and conferences?

Health

Do you have a bedtime? A time to turn off the TV? Do you expect your children to have healthy eating habits? Do you try to eat meals together as often as possible? Do you visit the dentist and the doctor when you are healthy or only when there is a problem? Do you set a healthy example? Do you remind your children to brush their teeth?

Worship and Prayer

Do you attend a worship service? Do you pray as a family and with your children? Do you look to God for guidance on this tough job of discipline? Do you attempt to follow the Ten Commandments?

There are probably other areas of your life in which you experience discipline and provide some external controls for your children. These are part of our daily life with our family. The decisions we make about how we spend our time and our resources reflect the limits and expectations that we provide.

We have choices to make about how we apply our limits. Each family will need to personalize their approach to external control and discipline. The most successful families combine humor, lots of expressions of love and warm, close physical contact with firm boundaries and consistent external controls. These children feel loved, cared for and protected by their limits. Sure, they will express frustration with them. Yes, they will be unhappy with them at times, but that is okay. They will also develop the character traits that are desirable for successful, happy adulthood.

Limits without love are punitive and harsh. They don't provide the safe haven that love provides. They create rebellion and anger and are unlikely to help your child develop in the way that you desire. While it is easy to feel frustrated and angry when your teen pushes the limits and challenges your choices, the more love you show with the limits, the easier it is on the whole family. Once limit setting turns into a shouting match, the parents have lost control, the teen has lost control, the limits are going to be lost in the anger, and the value of discipline is lost on everyone involved. The whole family is exhausted, and no one is any smarter.

The more talking and listening that a family can do with each other, the easier it is for everyone to live within and benefit from the limits that are necessary. If you spend time in casual conversation at the dinner table about right and wrong, about how you handled a frustration during the day, or about how everyone spends their time, then you set the framework for understanding when limits have to be set. If your child knows you think parents should be home when someone has a party, he is not surprised when you call his friend's house before a party to be sure someone is home. If you talk about favorite TV shows and some of the trouble the characters get into, your child has a way to understand your opinions on matters of right and wrong without your having to spell out directly for her what you believe in. If you have told your child you take your job of raising her seriously on other occasions, she understands when you say "no" to certain events or activities. (She may not like it, but she expects it from you.)

Think of your limits as a loving embrace: they should give a feeling of protection, not restriction; they should demonstrate love and tenderness, not harshness; they should guide and direct, helping our child become the adult he is capable of being. You can do this for your child—you are the parent, the competent adult who can show your child the way.

LEAD your Child in the Right Direction

If we can see the long view and provide limits, if we love our child more than life itself, if we accept the responsibility God gave us when He sent us this child, then we understand that our ultimate job is to help our child develop a saving relationship with the Lord Jesus Christ.

We are ultimately responsible for leading our child to God. While growing up in a Christian home is not enough for salvation, a Christian home has the obligation to introduce the children to a loving and saving God. We do this through our prayer, our worship and our involvement with our church community.

Establish habits that connect you and your family to God on a daily basis. Some of the prayer habits suggested in chapter 10 can help you with that. Talk about God casually at the dinner table and in the car. When you say, "Thank God," mean it. Don't be shy about telling your child you will pray for him, and then do it. Encourage your child to participate in the life of the church. Find something to do as a family that helps others. Stop taking the Lord's name in vain.

If you open your family life to God, He will come in. He comes in carefully and slowly. He meets you where you are as an individual and brings you where He wants you to be, but He is waiting for a sincere invitation from you. You can open the doors to the incredible positive changes God can bring into your lives. It takes only one member of the family to ask, to pray and to welcome God into his heart to begin the process of gradual transformation.

This is truly how the change happened in my family. We invited God in having no idea what to expect. Frankly, I was afraid of some of the changes and felt reluctant to allow God into my life. Would I have to give up soap operas? Would I have to begin to watch my language? Would I have to become one of those "church ladies" that people make fun of? I was afraid of all of this, but somehow God walked me through every change He made in me. As I changed, my family changed. Our conversation changed, and how we treated each other improved. I became a much better wife and mother—far from perfect, just better. The changes were gradual, not very painful at all. As a matter of fact, by the time each change was made, I was ready for it. I don't watch soap operas any more, but I also don't miss them. I don't use God's name in vain anymore. I've found more colorful phrases when I'm excited, happy or upset. I may have become one of those "church ladies" people make fun of, but that is okay with me. As a matter of fact, I consider it to be a statement of honor. What other kind of lady would I want to be ?

When I thank God at night for being at the center of my family, I am not always sure how He got there. He was once someone I gave very little consideration to, but He has become the most important element of my life and the life of my family. He quietly took over my heart, my mind and my life, and I couldn't be happier. He can do all of that for you also. He can improve the dynamics of your family life, changing the way you love each other, the way you treat each other, and the way your family views the world and your place in it. All you have to do is ask.

It was God's grace and mercy that brought Him into our lives. It was ALL Him: it had nothing to do with us. He opened our hearts, started our conversations, and introduced us to the activities that improve our relationship with Him (such as Bible study and church ministries). All we had to do was pray, invite Him in and wait for His miracles to happen to us. Oh, sure, I had to change some pretty ungodly habits like gossiping, wanting what my friend had, and expecting the world to revolve around my desires. But God helped me to do all that. I certainly wasn't capable of doing it on my own. All I had to do was pray and wait to respond to the direction God had planned for me and my family.

How do we lead our children to the right path for forever? We bring them to God, who is in charge of forever. He provided you with this wonderful (most of the time) child, and He can be with this child when you are not. He knows the beginning, the middle and the end of your child's story and has a wonderful plan for your child—a plan to prosper, not to harm; a plan to give your child a future and hope (Jeremiah 29:11).

Lead your child to God through His Son, who sacrificed His life for the your eternal life and your child's. Come boldly to the throne of grace. No one loves us as God does. We are His creation. His love makes parental love pale in comparison. Let's do everything we can to connect our child with the loving, merciful, grace-filled, forgiving presence of the Lord. It is the most permanent legacy we can leave to our beloved children—our greatest responsibility.

Things to Think About

- In what ways would your child say you show your love to him?
- Where do you provide limits for your child?
- Would your child identify you as a faithful person?
- Do you worship together as a family?
- Do you practice self-control in your personal behaviors (e.g., what you watch on TV, how much alcohol you use, how you conduct yourself in your relationships)?
- Do you tell your children, "I love you"?
- How do you protect your child?
- Are you more likely to obey the rules of our culture (what's popular to eat, drink, wear or drive), the rules of

mortal leaders (coaches, how to get ahead at work), or the rules of God?
- Are you satisfied with your prayer life?
- Are you comfortable with the boundaries you have for your child?

Things to Do

- Focus on God's presence in your life.
- Communicate with God every day regarding your blessings and struggles. Invite God into your daily living.
- Say, "I love you," to each other.
- Assess the amount of structure you provide as a parent. Add structure and discipline to the areas in which there are weaknesses. (Remember, we are all works in progress. Parents are also always learning, growing and developing. It is good to assess yourself every now and then and make any necessary changes. That is how we all become better parents.)
- Have conversations as a family, and listen to each other.
- Demonstrate your love.
- Stick to your limits.
- Introduce your child to God, and pray for her relationship with Him.

Scripture to Remember

- James 1:17 - Every good gift and every perfect gift is from above.
- Hebrews 4:16 - Let us therefore come boldly to the throne of grace, that we may obtain mercy and find grace to help in the time of need.
- Ephesians 4:32 - And be kind to one another, tender hearted, forgiving one another just as God, in Christ, forgave you.

- Jeremiah 29:12 - Then you will call upon me and go and pray to me, and I will listen to you.
- Isaiah 54:13 - All your children shall be taught by the Lord, and great shall be the peace of your children.
- Proverbs 16:20 - He who heeds the word wisely will find good, and whoever trusts in the Lord, happy is he.
- Psalm 145:18 - The Lord is near to all who call upon Him, to all who call upon Him in truth.
- Joshua 24:15 - Choose for yourselves this day whom you shall serve. . . . As for me and my house, we shall serve the Lord.

Endnotes

Endnotes

Chapter Two: FAMILY, Society's Cornerstone

1. John Rosemund, *Six Point Plan for Raising Happy, Healthy Children* (Kansas City: Andrews and McMeel, 1989), p. 8.

Chapter Three: DISCIPLINE, Trust Builder

1. Michael and Diane Medved, *Saving Childhood* (New York: Harper Collins, 1998), p. 217.
2. John Rosemund.

Chapter Four: DRINKING and Drug Use

1. Michael and Diane Medved, p. 125
2. Phyllis Ellickson, et.al., "Teenagers and Alcohol Misuse in the United States" *Addiction*, 1996, 91 (10) p. 1489.
3. Michael and Diane Medved, p. 126
4. Meg Meeker, *Restoring the Teenage Soul* (Traverse City, Mich.: McKinley & Mann, 1999), p. 88.
5. Michael Resnick, Ph. D., et. al. "Protecting Adolescents from Harm, " *JAMA*, 10 Sept 1997, Vol., 278, no. 10.

Chapter Five: PRESSURE, a Powerful Foe

1. Michael and Diane Medved, p. 140.

Chapter Six: TALKING and Listening

1. Realvision Facts and Figures about our TV Habit, Nelson Media Research 2000.

Chapter Eight: SEX, Delay or Pay

1. Center for Disease Control, "Sexually Transmitted Diseases," 2001, Report on STD's throughout the US, p. 18.
2. Ibid., p. 19.
3. Meg Meeker, p. 104.
4. "Sexual Health Today," Medical Institute of Austin, TX p. 76. (series of articles)
5. Meg Meeker, p. 104.
6. J. J. Apuzzle and M.A. Pelosi, "The New Salpingitis, Subtle Symptoms, Aggressive Management," *The Female Patient*, Nov 14, 1989.
7. CDC report, p. 20.
8. Ibid., p. 2.
9. Ibid., p. 20.
10. Ibid., p. 20
11. Ibid., p. 2.
12. Ibid.

Chapter Nine: POPULAR Culture's Influence

1. Realvision, Facts and Figures about our TV Habit.
2. Michael and Diane Medved, p. 5.
3. Ibid.
4. Archives of Pediatrics and Adolescent Medicine, January 2001.
5. Realvision, Facts and Figures about our TV Habit.

Chapter Eleven: BEING the Parent

1. Michael and Diane Medved, p. 140.
2. Centers for Disease Control Report, p. 2.
3. Lisa Collier Cool, "Secret Sex Lives of Children," *Ladies Home Journal*, March 2001, p. 157.
4. John Rosemund, p. 118.
5. Ibid.

Appendices

Appendix A

Further Questions Regarding Popular Culture Media

About Television

- How many of you like to watch TV?
- How many of you watch TV every day?
- How many of you watch at least three hours of TV every day?
- How many of you have a TV in your bedroom?
- How many of you have rules about TV? Rules about specific shows? Rules about logistics (e.g., no TV until the homework is done)? Rules about content (e.g., too violent, too much sex etc.)?
- What is your favorite TV program? (Ask 5 students.)

About Movies

- How many of you like to watch movies?
- How many of you watch most of your movies at home?
- How many of you have seen at least two R-rated movies in the past two months?
- How many of you are 17?
- How many of you have seen R-rated movies with your parents' permission?
- How many of you have seen R-rated movies with some one else's parents' permission but your parents probably wouldn't approve?
- How many of you have rules about movies? Based on content? Based on ratings? Based on other information your parents might have (e.g., if they have seen it them-selves, heard something or read reviews)?
- What is your favorite movie this year? (Ask 5 students.)

About Video Games

- How many of you like to play video games?
- How many of you play video games every day?
- How many of you spend more than one hour per day playing video games?
- How many of you have played your video games with your parents?
- How many of you have rules about video games? Related to ratings? Related to content? Related to logistics (e.g., homework done, specific amount of time)?

About Magazines

- How many of you like to read magazines?
- How many of you have favorite magazines that are about sports? Fashion? People? Video games? Computers? Music?
- How many of you have ever thought you were overweight? Convinced by the magazines?
- How many of you get your magazines by subscription?
- How many of you buy them at the store?

About Music

- How many of you like to listen to music?
- How many of you listen to more music than you watch TV?
- How many of you prefer to watch your music?
- How many of you watch your favorite music on MTV? BET? VHI?
- How many of you have rules about music related to content? Ratings? Logistics (e.g., loudness)?
- How many of your parents have ever read the lyrics to your music?
- Who is your favorite artist? (Ask 5 students.)

About Extracurricular Activities

- How many of you play a sport? For school? For your community?
- How many of you play unstructured sports, like pickup football?
- How many of you participate in drama or theatre?
- How many of you dance? With lessons?
- How many of you play an instrument?
- How many of you play your instrument in school only?
- How many of you take lessons outside of school?
- How many of you belong to a group or organization outside of school like scouts, explorers?
- How many of you belong to a group or organization in school like student government or math club?
- How many of you stay after school at least three days per week for something other than detention?
- How many of you go out to lessons or meetings in the evening at least two nights per week?
- How many of you go to lessons such as martial arts, voice, instrument, art, drama, hitting, batting?
- What activity have I missed?

About Family

- How many of you are the oldest child?
- How many of you are the youngest?
- How many of you are in the middle?
- How many of you live with your mom?
- How many of you live with your dad?
- How many of you live with half or step siblings?
- How many of you eat dinner with at least some of your family most nights?

Appendix B

Parent to Parent

When I have the opportunity to meet with parents, I ask them to write down their favorite parenting tip. As you can imagine, most of the tips revolve around our biggest issues, communication and discipline. Many of the tips I receive are common tips on consistency, time for talking and listening (the good day/ bad day tips are very popular), using your sense of humor and involving God in the life of your child. Please review this list and see if any of the ideas are new to you. Is there something in this list you just might try, anything you haven't thought of yourself, or a new way to look at an old problem? We as parents can influence each other to make decisions that are in the best interest of our children. You may have some favorite tips of your own. Pass them along. Consider starting a group in your church or school in which parents can support each other with advice, warmth and humor. Pray together with other parents. We started a moms prayer group at our school in which a few of us meet every Monday morning to pray for our school. We pray for each student, teacher and staff member, praying for specific requests but also praying in a general way for children who have sickness, money worries or family problems. We pray for everyone on behavior medication, for our teachers' patience and kindness, and we pray that our children will recognize the presence of God in their school days. We chat with each other before we pray and these few minutes (sometimes many minutes) restore us and encourage us to continue to "hang in there" when the times are tough. Moms in Touch International is a group that helps start mothers praying and provide prayer support for your group. See *When Mothers Pray,* by Cheri Fuller, in the recommended reading section (Appendix H) of the leader's guide for the video curriculum series *Sex as God's Gift*, page 54, for more information on this organization.

Whatever your opinion on feminism, we all must recognize how it changed our culture. Feminism started with small groups of women getting together to talk about how they thought things "should" be. Slowly, many of those "shoulds" became public discourse. We need to begin "familyism" in the same way. Get together with other parents you know, talk about positive steps you can take in your community to improve the lives of families working hard to do their best raising up their children. Begin to make these steps happen.

You won't be alone. At the end of every group I speak to, many parents come up to me to talk about how alone they feel in doing what is right for their children. There are always at least 5 people, even in a very small group, who tell me they feel like "the only ones" who are making the tough decisions (waiting issues, TV controls, decisions about appropriate social activities). So although you may feel alone, you are not. I hope these parenting ideas will help you to see the choices other families make to try to deal with complexities of family life.

Following are an assortment of the favorite parenting tips from real parents.

1. Don't be afraid to talk to your children.
2. Be a good listener.
3. Listen! But stand firm to your decision when you know it's been made for your child's well-being.
4. Begin communication with your children at the earliest age.
5. Build a relationship on trust as well as authority.
6. Make it a point to listen to your children at suppertime and let each of them talk about their day.

7. We play a game called "high-low" in which we talk about the best part of our day and the hardest part of our day.

8. Try to put myself in their spot and reminisce with stories of failures and triumphs of my own growing up.

9. Hear the other's side of the story before you react.

10. I have e-mailed my teenagers, and then they have time to read and think about what I have to say without a tone of voice or attitude (on either part). It works!!!

11. Yelling doesn't work.

12. Neither does nagging.

13. My child knows I was a teenager once.

14. Take each child out alone and sit down and really listen to him or her. It's a lot of fun!!

15. Discuss songs on the radio and who the artists are, what the song is about and whether it is real or not.

16. Spend time alone with each child every day even if it's only for a few minutes.

17. Whenever my child is ready to talk, I drop what I'm doing, sit or bend down, look her in the eyes and listen.

18. Reflective listening. Repeat what your child has said in slightly different words. This is also called therapeutic conversation.

19. Tell each child every day you love him.

20. Share, share, share.

21. Try to spend 10 minutes with your children the first time you see them (after school or work). Let them review their day.

22. Engage children in dialogue, asking questions, exploring challenges, feelings and sometimes finding answers.

23. Spend quiet time together, one on one.

24. Always take time in the day to listen to the children about their lives and thoughts, be it over a plate of freshly baked cookies or after a hug and kiss before bed time lights out.

25. Play a game.

26. At dinnertime we pray and always talk about each one of our days. We give each other advice. This keeps us all connected.
27. My children respond to a homemade snack on the counter. They sit down and start talking about what is on their minds. I do this when I think we've been too busy and need to catch up.
28. Don't overreact.
29. If you are quiet and listen, they will tell you everything.
30. Ask questions.
31. Try to listen to everyone's point of view when we have an argument.
32. Listen without commenting.
33. Sit down to a family meal each evening.
34. Give your children a chance to explain why
35. Listen with an open heart and mind and a closed mouth.
36. Find out how school went, how sports went, just talk for a while about the day.
37. At the end of each school year I treat my daughter and several friends to lunch in which we discuss the good and bad things of the school year.
38. Always have dinner together, pray and talk about our days.
39. Treat each child fairly, not necessarily equally.
40. Positive encouragement on jobs well done.
41. Lots of hugs (wherever they'll let you).
42. Respect down time. Everyone needs it. Have a chance to be on your own, quiet in a busy home.
43. Admit when you are wrong.
44. Bring a sense of wonder to your children. Show them the beauty in the world. Add fun, and there is no end to the joy!!
45. Give choices between two equally acceptable options.
46. We tell our children we love them daily; they try to "beat" us by telling us first!

47. Treat everyone the way you would want to be treated.
48. We laugh, act silly and have fun together.
49. Be there!
50. Allow your child to try anything, sports, music, teams, but always have them stick to it for the duration of the year before trying something else.
51. Expect the best, and you will get it.
52. If you are going to do something, do the right thing and do it right.
53. Try to treat your child as a person that you love.
54. Stay interested in their lives.
55. "Let me think about it first."
56. Talk about the long-term view of the problem.
57. Be affectionate with your children.
58. Don't do for your children what they could do for themselves.
59. Snuggle.
60. I hold my child when she is totally out of control. I rock her and hug her and help her to get focused again. I talk low and have her try to look in my eyes.
61. Recognize that your child is not a carbon copy of yourself.
62. Talk in the car.
63. Take walks with the new dog; we have talking time and exercise, too.
64. Attend whatever they participate in—sports, concerts, recitals.
65. Go out to lunch.
66. We learned figure skating together.
67. Cook together.
68. Big puzzles: do them together.
69. Go on a picnic in the woods.
70. I tuck all my children into bed, even my teenage son. I kiss them and tell them I love them.
71. Sit with your teen as s/he lies in bed at night. They talk more openly.

72. I kiss my children goodnight no matter how our evening or day has gone. It reinforces that I still love them, no matter what.
73. I do a job that I want them to do and then try to show them how to do it themselves.
74. Spend homework time together.
75. I leave my children a little personal note every now and then.
76. We are consistent. My children know exactly what to expect.
77. When angry, wait for 2 to 3 minutes before screaming. Think about what you want to say before you say it.
78. Try to reduce your level of anger before you discuss a situation.
79. Be open to your child's problems. If they admit they did something, thank them for being honest. Discuss. Keep communication open for future surprises. There can still be punishment, but let them know that you are being more lenient because they were honest.
80. When your child does something wrong, let them know there will be consequences, and stick to them.
81. For consequences: take or keep something that they really want or want to do from them.
82. Don't give in to "everyone else can do it." That doesn't make it right.
83. Laugh when you are angry.
84. When my children were teenagers I was strict. My children knew who the boss was. It didn't seem to hurt them; they are all well-rounded adults.
85. For problem resolution: turn to each other, hold hands, state in "I" form what the problem is. This helps to teach communication and leads to effective problem resolution.
86. Study hall between 7-9 p.m. No phone calls are allowed, no socializing on line. Once homework is done, the children can read. They usually want to be with us! The parents!

87. Family meetings.
88. When I say no I mean it.
89. After disciplining, I always tell my son I love him.
90. Let children experience the consequences of their actions.
91. "What would God want you to do?"
92. When we reach a standstill in discussion, we write out thoughts then meet and share these thoughts. We ask for solutions from our children on how we can solve the issue at hand.
93. Look at the good things your child does, and tell them you like the way they are behaving.
94. Play tennis or go fishing to spend time with each other, listening.
95. Your child has to be responsible for his or her actions.
96. I give myself time-out when I am frustrated and angry.
97. Don't allow demeaning words.
98. When my children are fighting, I try to stay out of their argument unless someone is bleeding. I do repeat what they tell me so they can figure out a solution for themselves.
99. I try very hard not to take my teenage boys' moodiness to heart and love him unconditionally. This is hard so I send him e-mails and love notes.
100. Know where your child is and whom he or she is with: know their friends.
101. Always call the parent of any house your child is going to.
102. We have friends to our house A LOT!! That way we get to know them.
103. Stay interested in their lives.
104. Tickle time.
105. Give the right example.
106. Help out with homework; don't do it, but help.
107. "I know you know this already but let me be the mother for a minute."

108. Our family life is God and "other" centered.
109. Keep outside influences at arm's distance, and make the final choice on your children's right and wrong yourself.
110. Don't forget authority and discipline.
111. Trust your instincts; reel your child in whenever you have to.
112. Realize that you are your child's parent, not buddy; let them know you are secure in this role (even when they are not).
113. Don't spoil your children by giving them everything they want. They will appreciate this later.
114. I have learned the hard way not to let a child with a strong personality gain too much control in the family.
115. Take charge; be the parent.
116. We are not afraid to say "no" to our children.
117. Be firm. Follow through on your threats. Do not take back a punishment.
118. Be honest and firm. Provide good discipline.
119. Don't flip out or over react.
120. Let your children know you mean business.
121. I let my teen have the last word. Oh, this is so hard.
122. Try always to keep your sense of humor.
123. We always hug after an argument.

Scripture Index

Scripture Index

Additional Resources

Additional Video Resources
by Mary Ronan

Sex as God's Gift video curriculum

Mary Ronan talks straight and plain. Kids love her,
listen to her and respond. Produced especially for 14 and 15 year olds, these programs
help them think through in advance decisions
related to sex. This series challenges young
people to understand sex as a valuable gift,
something special and meaningful and not as
a recreational sport.

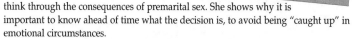

Special emphasis is given to avoidance
of sexual activity before marriage. Mary presents the facts in a straightforward, honest way
that teens relate to and respect. She helps them
think through the consequences of premarital sex. She shows why it is
important to know ahead of time what the decision is, to avoid being "caught up" in
emotional circumstances.

Our youth receive false and misleading information about sex from many
sources, especially the media. Television and movies give young people a distorted
and unhealthy understanding of sex. These six programs will help youth understand
the beauty, importance, and reasons for Biblical morality: (1) Making Good Decisions,
(2) STDs and Pregnancy, (3) The Reality of Teen Pregnancy, (4) Sexuality is a Gift, (5)
Relationships, and (6) Common Questions Teens Have. **Along with the six programs
are teacher's guide, student worksheets, and an additional book and video set enti-
tled** *Raising Your Children in an Ungodly World* **(described below).**

Curriculum kit, **#4467,** $79.99

Raising Your Children in an Ungodly World

Do you find it difficult to relate to your teenager? Mary
Ronan can help. In speaking to thousands of teens each year,
Mary has discovered the three things that most concern our
youth today: pressure, drugs and alcohol, and sex. In this program Mary explores how the media and popular culture
assault our youth and offers parents guidance on how to talk
to teens and help them deal with these influences. Her suggestions are built around three major themes: love them, lead them, and limit
them. Here is practical advice that will help you to help your teenager.

Video & book, **#4469,** $24.99   Book alone, #4535, $9.99

To order, or for more information, contact Vision Video:
1-800-523-0226 or www.visionvideo.com

Chastity Video Programs

Sex, Love and Relationships
Straight Talk with Pam Stenzel

Today's youth have not been told the whole truth about the consequences of sexual activity, experimentation and permissiveness. Teenagers love Pam Stenzel because she tells it to them straight, mincing no words in showing how the pervasive sexual permissiveness of our culture is a deceptive trap. Every young person should have the benefit of the hard-hitting reality check in this award-winning four-part series. Pam's message is helping thousands avoid disastrous consequences of unwise choices.

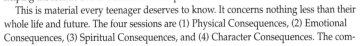

This is material every teenager deserves to know. It concerns nothing less than their whole life and future. The four sessions are (1) Physical Consequences, (2) Emotional Consequences, (3) Spiritual Consequences, and (4) Character Consequences. The complete curriculum package includes four video programs, 135 minutes total; comprehensive leader's guide; and reproducible student handouts.

Also in an abridged version!

In this abridged version of the series, Pam offers practical help for some of the important choices teens must face. (Video only) 55 minutes, **#4280,** $19.99

Complete curriculum package, **#4279,** $49.99

Public school edition (*Time to Wait for Sex*), 60 minutes, **#99347,** $19.99.

Sex & Love: What's a Teenager to Do?

In this dynamic, high-energy presentation, Mary Beth Bonacci talks to teens about the "do's" of chastity. Using Scripture and humorous, down-to-earth examples from teenage life, she shows that chastity is more than just abstinence — chastity is active. It's about loving in a relationship the way that God intended.

60 minutes, **#4145,** $19.99   (Public school edition, **#4181**)

Life: It's a Gift and a "Class" Project
A powerful drama that helps teens see it like it is

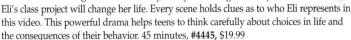

This intense film deals with abortion, casual sex and teen relationships. As God created life in the Garden of Eden, Eli, a teacher at Eden High School, creates life in his basement. He will give the responsibility to his students to care for the lives he creates. Some will pass; others will fail. One will abort the life he has given her. For Emily, a 17-year-old high school junior, Eli's class project will change her life. Every scene holds clues as to who Eli represents in this video. This powerful drama helps teens to think carefully about choices in life and the consequences of their behavior. 45 minutes, **#4445,** $19.99

Other Teen Issue Videos

More Chastity Programs - Ellen Marie

Ellen Marie is a dynamic speaker helping teenagers make healthy life-long choices. She is founder of Youth Support, Inc., in Minneapolis, MN.

Teen Relationships & Sexual Pressure - Jason Evert and Ellen Marie share real-life stories from teens with whom they have dealt. Helps teens understand why chastity is beneficial and gives them tools to live out this choice. #4537, $19.99

Hard Questions, Straight Answers - Jason takes the guys aside, and Ellen Marie takes the girls aside to answer frank, direct questions they have about sex from a Biblical perspective. Jason w/guys, #4538, $14.99; Ellen Marie w/girls, #4539, $14.99.

Reality in Relationships *for teens* - Teens will find this program realistic, captivating, and educational. This powerful chastity program filmed in a high school helps teens to understand what creates quality relationships, the practical reasons for chastity, and why the guidelines regarding the gift of sexuality in the Bible are for teenagers' benefit. 45 min., #99457, $19.99

Parenting the Teenager *for parents* - Proven techniques on how parents can talk to pre-teens and teens about dating, sex, drugs, and other issues. 60 min., #99456, $19.99

Drugs & Alcohol

Out of the Night - True, dramatic presentation. Stephen was a pilot for a multimillionaire friend, who turned out to be a major cocaine transporter. He was arrested, pled guilty, and received a five-year sentence. In prison his life was transformed when he found the Lord, resulting in a commitment to help teens avoid the same mistakes. 45 min., #4168, $19.99. Also, in *Arrington Live*, Stephen shares his story live with teens. 45 min., #4170, $19.99.

Alone in the Dark - Giving in to peer pressure, 17-year-old Tasha Grant goes to a party and gets drunk and takes the wheel, unaware of the life-threatening danger ahead. This suspenseful drama depicts the lethal dangers of alcohol and shows how our actions have consequences. Includes Biblical study guide. 27 min., #4138, 19.99

Pop Culture & the Media

Sound & Fury - This program examines the power of music and demonstrates the profound implications of this addiction — from organizing thought patterns in the brain to helping power the engine of the sexual revolution. An eye-opening journey into the heart of popular music culture. Parental discretion advised. 45 minutes, #5797, $19.99 Also, *Music to Die For* is a fast-paced exposé of today's music with numerous mainstream artists and Christian artists. Parental discretion advised. 40 min., #1132, $19.99.

They Lied to Us - This emotional and moving video poignantly explores the lives of several young people who "bought the lies" of society through television, movies, magazines, and music — and suffered the consequences. A direct and honest approach for young people. 45 min., #99765, $19.99

Parents & Teens

Dear Distant Dad - Teenagers open up their hearts with a rare and raw honesty to reveal the devastating hurt they feel inside when they cannot lovingly connect with their dads. Great for youth, dads, or families. 23 min., #4076, $14.99